# ANTIQUES ROADSHOW

# ANTIQUES ROADSHOW
## HOW TO SPOT A FAKE

EDITED BY LARS THARP

BOXTREE

First published in 1999 by Boxtree,
an imprint of Macmillan Publishers Ltd,
25 Eccleston Place,
London, SW1W 9NF
and Basingstoke

Associated companies throughout the world

Created by Leapfrog Press Ltd.
Editor Slaney Begley
Art Editor Adrienne Hutchinson

ISBN 0 7522 1791 7

Copyright © Boxtree 1999

Based on the BBC television programme *Antiques Roadshow*
*Antiques Roadshow* is a trademark of the BBC and is used under licence

1 3 5 7 9 8 6 4 2

A CIP catalogue record for this book is available from the British Library

Colour Reproduction by Aylesbury Studios Ltd. Bromley.
Printed and bound in Great Britain by Butler and Tanner, Frome.

'Some disguised Deceits do
counterfeit Truth so perfectly
that not to be taken in by them
would be an error of Judgment.'

La Rochefoucauld, Maxims, 1665

# CONTENTS

# FOREWORD

The beautiful Saida is gazing down at me. Saida is a 19th-century French bronze of a stunning young woman, wearing a headscarf, casually tied at the back. Her hair is falling over her forehead and the gaze in her eyes is wistful. She bears the signature of the sculptor E. Villani and the official stamp of the Société des Bronzes de Paris. Saida has all the appearances of authenticity but, alas, Saida is a fake.

The story of Saida is a fascinating one. Some 20 years ago, I set about tracing the origin of fake French bronzes which were then flooding the market. Eventually, I was tipped off that there was a talented young forger working in a disused garage in Essex. Much to my surprise, he readily agreed to talk about what he was doing. Better than that, he demonstrated his technique. He had invested in an original 19th-century bronze of Saida. He then covered it in fine plaster and made a very accurate mould. Using that mould, he made dozens of identical copies in hard resin. Next, he filled the hollow cast with lead shot and sealed the base. Finally, he sprayed the cast with bronze paint. After the paint had dried, his copy was virtually indistinguishable from the original. He then sold these copies to the antiques trade for £25 each. Unscrupulous dealers, knowing that these were fake bronzes, passed them off to unsuspecting collectors for around £1,000. It became a big business and many people paid a great deal of money in the mistaken belief that they were buying genuine 19th-century bronzes. Saida is my own souvenir of an encounter with a forger.

The image of the forger as a loveable rogue able to expose the fallibility of experts and fool the untutored layman is an unjustified and misleading one. Fakes and forgeries are intended to deceive, they are a fraud. Although we might quietly admire the undoubted skills of the forgers we should not be lulled into regarding their activities as anything other than a criminal deception.

I am delighted that this superbly illustrated *Antiques Roadshow* guide, written by the programme's experts and edited by Lars Tharp, will help you to detect the many fakes that lurk in the muddier waters of the antiques world. The wise advice within these pages will help you to understand why the two words you should always bear in mind when investing in antiques are *caveat emptor* – buyer beware.

Hugh Scully
Presenter
*Antiques Roadshow*

# Introduction

## by Lars Tharp

*'And as a fake I shall, of course, excite more interest that the genuine article.'*

*Professor Anthony Blunt (Keeper of the Queen's Pictures and Russian spy)
in Alan Bennett's* A Question of Attribution *(1989)*

There's something thrilling about a fake. Like a secret agent it can worm its way into the holiest of holies – a private collection, a great national museum or even into the pages of an authoritative publication. Its intentions are subversive, its simple disguise – outward appearance, provenance – its passport. It seems, but isn't. It accosts and rubs shoulders with alleged 'old friends', those genuine members of a club through whose doors, with collar high, it passes as 'a regular'. Once inside no one is safe. Neighbour mistrusts neighbour. Which is the fake – the newcomer or perhaps the once trusted old friend? Many years may pass before it is exposed. Meanwhile the fake is licensed to kill. It kills reputations. Eminent experts are thrown on to fatally false trails, promising careers are blindfolded and lead by the nose up an empty alley. Thus Piltdown Man – the supposed 'missing link' that was in fact made up from a medieval human cranium planted alongside an artificially aged ape jaw – fooled and distracted a whole generation of anthropologists; and later, in the 1980s, the phony *Hitler Diaries* bludgeoned the reputations of over-credulous professors. It's a violent business.

For those of us gawping from below as these experts perform their high-wire acts, juggling fakes and originals, there's always a certain frisson when an act begins to falter. While full of admiration for the boffin who can tell Bow from Bogus, who can deny the satisfaction we feel when experts are fooled? We take a certain consolation in our own ignorance. As La Rochefoucauld said, 'If we had no faults we should not find so much enjoyment in the discomfiture of others'.

*Telling a genuine maiolica dish, such as the example above, from one of the many excellent fakes on the market, has defeated many an expert over the years.*

## What is a Fake?

How does a fake differ from a forgery, a facsimile, a reproduction or a straightforward copy? In *How to Spot a Fake* the word 'fake' is used in its broadest sense, namely a work of art intended to deceive. Strictly speaking, however, a 'fake' (as defined by the *Oxford English Dictionary*) is something which has been 'faked up' or modified from its original appearance, whether by addition or subtraction. It has been altered in order to deceive. The modification may be elaborate: a massive Chinese Chippendale mirror, supposedly late 18th-century but in fact an assembly of genuine 18th-century mirrors chopped up and reassembled into one completely 'new' creation. It may be crude: a stuffed trout partially coated in rabbit fur (the 1970s Canadian furry fish hoax). It may be straightforward: the addition of a 'signature' on a genuine Old Master sketch. Or it may be subtle: the sly removal of an honest factory mark in the hope that its absence will lead the buyer to attribute to a better factory. Thus the marks of Samson, a Paris porcelain factory originally making honest replacements for old broken dinner services (*see pages 34–5 and 44–5*) have frequently been removed and other marks substituted.

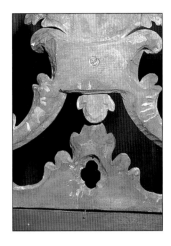

*The back of an object can often reveal more about its history than the front.*

A forgery, meanwhile, is a work which, from the very outset was intended to deceive. It is dishonest in all its parts. A potter firing a facsimile of someone else's mark or signature into his own pot is making a forgery. In the case of the Fetherstone Prison 'Bernard Leach' lookalikes (*see pages 48–9*), the rogue potters could not deny that, from the very outset, they intended deception, impressing replicas of Leach's St Ives Pottery seal marks into the still wet clay. Perhaps the case might have gone differently had they used the ruse of certain 18th-century Staffordshire potters. When imitating Wedgwood, competitors often marked pieces indistinctly or with a name which was close to but arguably different from the original: VEDGWOOD, WEDGWOO or WEDGEWOOD. In a court of law they could have pointed to the deliberate mis-spelling of the name. In fired, signed clay a charge of forgery is difficult to deny.

On paper it becomes more difficult. When a number of paintings signed Samuel Palmer were revealed as the work of a living artist, Tom Keating (*see pages 88–9*), the evidence for forgery seemed clear. But a subsequent BBC television programme showed Keating at his easel, painting while apparently under the spiritual direction of the long-dead Samuel Palmer – a sort of painting-seance. Keating claimed not to have signed his 'Palmers'. 'It wasn't me, guv'. If his inspirational trance was genuine, his works would not be forgeries but fakes that had been subsequently altered (the signature) with a view to deceive. With paper or canvas, where the time of signature cannot easily be demonstrated, it is difficult to prove forgery. So let us simply call them fakes.

*Arch forgers such as Han van Meegeren have become folk heroes once their exploits have become general knowledge.*

In the celebrated case of Han van Meegeren (*see pages 84–7*), where genuinely old paintings on original stretchers were skimmed down to the bare canvas, then repainted with a new image, varnished and artificially aged, the result is a fake: an already existing object (the old canvas) has been altered. Likewise, genuine undecorated 18th-century Sèvres plates sold off in the white and decorated in the 19th century are fakes.

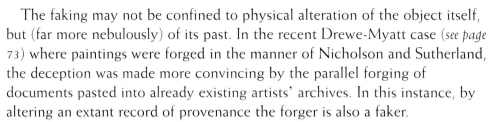

*The signatures of famous people are often produced using an autopen. Neither forgeries nor copies, they are still worth very little when compared to a handwritten note.*

The faking may not be confined to physical alteration of the object itself, but (far more nebulously) of its past. In the recent Drewe-Myatt case (*see page 73*) where paintings were forged in the manner of Nicholson and Sutherland, the deception was made more convincing by the parallel forging of documents pasted into already existing artists' archives. In this instance, by altering an extant record of provenance the forger is also a faker.

A smaller London auction room was recently given a rather grizzly relic for sale. Presented to the expert as Rasputin's Penis, it came with a seemingly watertight provenance, having (according to the owner) been cherished and handed down from its original owner via a member of the Romanov family. It came in its own padded box. Though somewhat grey and shrivelled, it was about 20 cm (8 in) long, a most remarkable thing. His suspicions aroused on several counts, the expert submitted the organ for forensic analysis. Several days later it was pronounced as being a perfectly genuine sea cucumber. The 'impeccable provenance' (with browned letters and documents) turned out to be mere fantasy and the phony phallus was withdrawn. With nothing but a story, a sea cucumber (which cannot be accused of being a fake or a forgery) becomes a hoax.

These examples show the overlap between fake and forgery, which is why, in the following pages we have lumped the two together, along with copies, facsimiles, replicas and reproductions. The simple fact is this: irrespective of the original maker's intentions, all can be used by their owners in an attempt to deceive a buyer, collector, museum or television expert. Only when passed with a view to deceive do they become fakes.

## Avoiding a Fake

For a fake to change hands it must appear in the marketplace, unless a private deal is made between individuals. At this point the owner may or may not know that the object is a dud. If he or she says 'I really don't know what it is' or 'I don't normally deal in these things', you should assume there's something wrong. No one in the antiques business will sell something before satisfying themselves that they are not selling the one piece they could have retired on, if only they'd spotted it. A Thai bronze sold in a furniture shop with no other bronzes, or a Chinese Ming-style blue-and-white dish sold at an open-air market where there is no other porcelain, should be treated with the utmost caution – it is probably a forgery. While making a recent series of *Antiques Inspectors* we saw a blue-and-white dish, a 16th-century forgery, with a price tag of £800, halfway between its actual value (£40) and a value if genuine (£1,500). Beware of halfway prices.

If you're happy to proceed, check what the label or catalogue description says and make sure that all the information given appears verbatim on any

*Items such as this Chinese snuff bottle, which would be unfamiliar to most people, can easily trip up the unwary buyer or seller.*

receipt along with any other verbal attributions, embellishments or assurances given by the person from whom you are buying. If the purchase later turns out to be factually misrepresented (whether or not on purpose) you will at least have a strong case for a refund.

When buying at auction, check out the catalogue for the auctioneer's definitions of origin and authorship. These are usually set out in the front of the catalogue, in stages: from the base camp of harmless copy to the peak of an undisputed original, with several increments of attribution in between. Treat anything with less than a categorical attribution (that is with the full name of the artist, factory or publisher, and a date) as a potential copy, a lookalike, fake or forgery even though nowhere in the genteel auction house will such common terms be used. Before the auction takes off take note of the cataloguer's emergency exits: they are clearly marked 'follower of', 'school of', 'in the manner of', 'in the style of' or just plain 'after' J. Reynolds – usually meaning 'a long time after'. Look out also for the terse 'bears signature', 'bears inscription' or 'signed' J. Reynolds – generally short for 'signed, but nothing like the work of' J. Reynolds.

Just occasionally, of course, the cataloguing may work in your favour: where an artist such as Van Dyke is known to have had a whole studio of assistants, churning out paintings on a production line, a picture carefully catalogued as 'school of' turns out to be by the master. Such coups are exceptional and require some luck and much expertise.

*Clarice Cliff's pottery is currently being reproduced, completely legitimately, by Wedgwood. Make sure, therefore, that you know whether you are buying an original piece or a reproduction.*

# Dirty Tricks: Age, Wear and Patina

Dirt is an easy aging aid, covering a forgery in 'years' of grime. The English artist William Hogarth poured scorn on those collectors who, clamouring for Old Masters to fill the walls and galleries of their opulent new houses, were duped by an artificial crusty brown patina. They really thought that paintings improved with age and patina. Hogarth's print *Time Smoking a Picture* (1761) depicts Old Father Time sitting at an easel, his scythe slashing the canvas while a further simulation of age is induced by billowing clouds of smoke puffed from his clay pipe. Technology changes: 200 years later Han van Meegeren coated his pictures in phenolformaldehyde resin and baked them in a medium oven at 105°C (221°F) for two hours or until 'done'. The resultant surface kept experts and analysts busy for years.

Though ageing techniques have become more sophisticated, some are still pretty basic. Travellers returning from the Far East clutching ancient-looking pottery tomb figures, ritual bronzes and archaic jades are likely to have bought modern pieces aged by several months' immersion in a local cess-pit.

Also, beware of wear. When looking at a supposedly old weathered or worn piece of furniture always ask yourself, 'Where would everyday wear

*Use your common sense when examining an object for wear and tear. A leather golf ball, for instance, would be stained with grass and would be worn where it had been hit.*

*Restoration work can effect the price of a piece dramatically. This 18th-century paste brooch is worth around £1,500 – as long as the mount has not been repaired or converted.*

*Sometimes a perfectly genuine object will be altered to increase its value. The figure above was originally an ashtray, but has been converted into a car mascot.*

have occurred? What patterns might constant use induce?' If the marks of time appear as much in the nooks and crannies of the piece as on the more exposed surfaces, something is wrong. Or if the scuffs and scratches on the base of a glass all run in one or two directions, be very suspicious. Get out the magnifying glass. If minute stress-cracks emanate from worm-holes, worm-holes they ain't – they have been put there with an awl or sharp spike.

## Condition and Age

And while looking so closely at surfaces back and front we should also watch out for restoration. After all, if an object is incorrectly sold to you as 'in mint condition', but turns out to be cleverly repaired or restored, it comes pretty close to having been faked. There's nothing wrong with having an object sympathetically restored, but the purchaser should know.

Nearly all old violins have at one stage been damaged and restored (*see pages 156–7*). Most professional violinists send off their instruments for regular check-ups when the restorer carefully lifts off the whole front of the violin for servicing the interior. In days gone by this gave unscrupulous restorer-dealers plenty of opportunity to remove a minor maker's label, pasting in a better one in its place. From fiddles to furniture, regard with suspicion any label that seems to have been tampered with, its edges frayed and re-pasted. Ask yourself, 'Under what circumstances might the label have been moved?' Then there are the forged labels, specially printed for insertion into anonymous instruments. Not so long ago Sotheby's sold a whole batch of Stradivarius labels. Where are they today?

## Fake or Genuine: Does It Matter?

'If it's so difficult to tell if it's fake, if the original and the copy are so close why worry? You should like the object for its own merits, not for some chain of past ownership. Good luck to the faker, I say.'

There's a grain of truth in this view. Yes, we ought to appreciate a book, a painting or a piece of furniture on its own terms. The history of a work of art should not get in the way of our looking at it critically, for its aesthetic qualities. But those who preach art for art's sake make one very big, mistaken assumption, that what we see is there, before our very eyes. This is not the case. Like religious relics (the medieval world was awash with fragments of the True Cross), works of art carry a value of association. In varying degrees they are relics through whose genuine association we see something beyond.

A pen that belonged to President John F. Kennedy or Princess Diana will always realize far more at auction than a similar pen that belonged to a nobody. 'Association', 'provenance', 'aura', call it what you will, can be tangibly more valuable than the bare object itself. Our knowledge, what we bring to the object, is a major factor in what the object is.

So authenticity determines how we see. A child in a museum sees a small dish covered in a crackled bluish glaze. Something she says she could have made. But when a label tells us it is an exceptionally rare *ruyi*-ware scholar's brush washer, made for the imperial palace during the Song dynasty (960–1279 AD), we see the piece differently. So differently that some collectors, once assured of its authenticity, would pay a million pounds for it.

*Early bookbindings were often considered dull by later collectors, and many were replaced with beautifully executed, but false, covers. The example above is a genuine 14th-century binding.*

## Revelations

No programme on television demonstrates this bringing-to-the-object better than the BBC *Antiques Roadshow*, a programme where the expert identifies and decodes an heirloom, and where the owner's own story also brings a piece to the jigsaw. Professing little knowledge of her pottery owl's origins, and liking it even less, the owner tells Henry Sandon that she has been using it for flowers (*see page 42*). Henry raises an eyebrow, pauses, and tells her that her 'vase' is a drinking vessel, made around the year 1700. She is then given a valuation in tens of thousands of pounds. For the owner, for 14 million UK viewers and for an audience around the world the 'I-wouldn't-give-it-house-room' object changes, not physically, of course, but in the way we look at it.

More recently in Torquay (1999), a lady clutching two broken porcelain bowls moved gradually to the front of the ceramics queue. On closer inspection the bowls were found to be fused, one inside the other. The porcelain was clearly 20th century, Japanese, and of a mass-produced 'kitchen' quality. I instantly diagnosed the group as a production reject, a 'kiln-waster', a jumble of badly fired vessels which, on emerging from a disastrous potter's firing, had been thrown out onto the factory spoil-heap. I was wrong. 'What made you bring these along?' I asked. Her husband had served in the Royal Navy and visited Japan in 1945, just after the dropping of atomic bombs on Hiroshima and Nagasaki. From Hiroshima's ruins he had retrieved these pathetic pieces, fused together by the flash of that nuclear fire-ball. Like the famous half-melted watch, searing steel hands to its face the very second the bomb had burst, these simple bowls had welded the moment the world had changed. From being a little worthless heap, this deeply poignant ceramic wreck had suddenly 'transformed' into an exhibit worthy of any museum.

*Terrible disappointments as well as great discoveries can take place on a Roadshow. Imagine taking along your treasured silver sauceboat, only to find that it has been converted from a ladle.*

In the following pages experts from the *Antiques Roadshow* bring together just a few examples of their favourite 'secret agents', subversive works that at some time have deceived and lied their way into someone's heart. In exposing these imposters our hope is to offer an insight into the way we look at objects – and how we choose our friends.

# POTTERY, PORCELAIN AND GLASS

The study of ceramics is an endless study of imitations. Just when you think you've learnt to recognize a particular factory, potter, style or period, along comes a familiar-looking vase, plate or figure: the pattern or shape is distinctive and immediately you say: 'Aha! Japanese. Kakiemon, *circa* 1700'. You turn it over (which you should have done in the first place) and find a European mark. Whoops! If you were buying, your mistaken 'identification' would have been expensive. As a collector your investment is a bubble waiting to burst. And as a cataloguer in a major auction house, both your job and the company's reputation are at stake.

Where copies of copies abound, with potential errors waiting around every corner, how do you spot a fake? Be Sceptical of First Appearances – those features that immediately engage the eye and seduce you with the pleasure of recognition. The faker's front line is usually armed with three major weapons: pattern, shape (or form) and, not least, the mark or signature. All of these features are easily copied. Learn to duck such attacks on your intellect. Arm yourself with a constantly growing arsenal of Experience and Memory by visiting museums and attending auctions (where you are allowed to handle). Fill your mind with a map of the territory; learn just how much has been copied over 10,000 years.

Our chosen examples reflect not only the range seen on a typical *Antiques Roadshow*, but also a few fabulously rare pieces which just might be lurking in the queue. Just as the expert must always be on his or her guard not to overlook the modest-looking 'ashtray' that turns out to be Song dynasty and worth £100,000, he or she should be equally careful not to go before a television audience with a priceless piece of blue-and-white, which later turns out to be Taiwan – the Ming with a sting.

# MING VASE

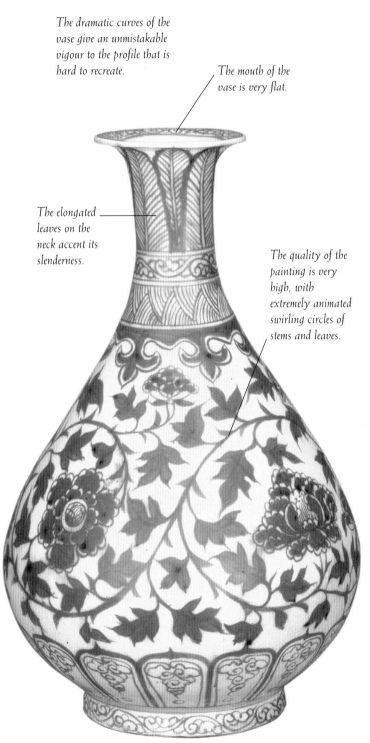

*The dramatic curves of the vase give an unmistakable vigour to the profile that is hard to recreate.*

*The mouth of the vase is very flat.*

*The elongated leaves on the neck accent its slenderness.*

*The quality of the painting is very high, with extremely animated swirling circles of stems and leaves.*

The Chinese discovered the secret of making porcelain in the Tang dynasty (618–906). Over the next 400 years, countless improvements were made in the body and glaze until, in the first quarter of the 14th century, during the Yuan dynasty (1279–1368), underglaze blue was developed (*see page 24*). The Yuan dynasty fell and the Ming took over. The first Ming emperor Hongwu (1368–98) decreed that the flourishing trade in porcelain should stop. It obviously did not, as the edict was issued several times during his time on the throne. Porcelain continued to be made for domestic purposes and for diplomatic presents and towards the end of his reign, more copper red than blue-and-white was being made. Underglaze copper red, discovered at much the same time as underglaze blue, is much more difficult to control in the kiln and often turns mushroom grey or silvery. Underglaze blue suffered from a different problem; lack of control of the blue led to an effect known as 'heaping and piling', where the cobalt oxide swims up through the glaze and appears as black dots or patches. Originally a firing fault, it is now thought to add vigour to the painting.

Today, 'Ming' has become almost synonymous with the word 'porcelain'. Early on, large dishes, bowls and vases were the main production, usually painted with dragons or scrolling flowers, particularly peony. The most common vase form is the *yuhuchunping*, a generously swelled body with trumpet neck painted in underglaze blue or red (*see left*). The exact shape of the vase should be studied as it is an object lesson in how a copy (*see opposite*) rarely has the same 'life' as the original. Here the profile of the belly has become gentler, the neck shorter and stumpier and the mouth less flat.

The reign of the Ming dynasty that carries most prestige as far as porcelain is concerned is that of Xuande (1426–35). At this period, the quality of

*Genuine Hongwu copper red vase, late 14th century, 32 cm (12⅝ in) tall, £1.3 million*

# Modern copy of a Ming vase

the potting, painting and the blue itself has never been equalled. The modern copy is based on the earlier Hongwu copper red, but is here in blue and carries the six-character mark of Xuande. It was made in China, probably at the so-called Ming village in Jingdezhen, about 10 years ago. It was bought for £60 at an 'antiques' fair from a stallholder who claimed that he had no idea what it was. Had such a piece existed a million pounds would have been more realistic.

*The spearhead border is larger than one might expect and the stiff leaves on the neck, too short.*

*The profile, with its stumpy neck and gentle curves, lacks the vigour and liveliness of the original.*

*The calligraphy on the base of the vase is very stiff and the character* nian *is poorly formed. A copy quite often fails on the quality of the script, which, like English handwriting, has varied through the ages. It is therefore important to learn the different styles.*

*The circle of the stem is badly drawn, the flower head is not central and the stem is flat at the bottom.*

## Marks

Six-character mark of the emperor applied to pieces made for his and court use. It reads *ta Ming Xuande nianzhi* (made in the reign of the Great Ming Emperor Xuande).

| | |
|---|---|
| de | ta |
| nian | Ming |
| zhi | Xuan |

大明宣德年製

*The foot is too large in proportion to the body.*

*Imitation Hongwu vase, late 20th century, £60*

# CHENGHUA PERIOD CHICKEN CUP

*The Chenghua clay has a slightly darker tone than the Kangxi porcelain.*

*This coffee-coloured edge on the foot ring, where the glaze was wiped prior to firing, is distinctive of Ming porcelains.*

*The yellow has a smoky, almost brown quality.*

*The iron-red outlining on the plumage is almost brick red.*

Each of these two cups is a mere 7.5 cm (3 in) wide. Both are decorated with the same simple pattern of cocks, hens and chicks foraging among rocks and plants. The example on the left was made in the Ming dynasty during the reign of the emperor Chenghua (1465–87). Meanwhile, the cup on the right is a late 17th- or early 18th-century copy. Though perhaps not very different in appearance, the variation in value is significant: the 15th-century original was sold by Sotheby's in Hong Kong in 1999 when it became 'pound for pound' perhaps the costliest small piece of clay in the world, fetching HK$29 million (£2.3 million). Though a copy, its Qing lookalike might be worth up to a tenth of the original, still 'a tidy sum'. With so large a margin at stake on two such similar pieces it is clearly important for auctioneer and collector alike to know the differences. So how do we distinguish Ming from Qing?

Some 250 years before the first successful European attempts to make a hard-paste porcelain, the Chinese were producing finely potted, flawless white porcelain decorated in underglaze metallic oxides as well as overglaze enamel colours. For a few very special pieces destined for the emperor himself, a painting style was invented combining underglaze and overglaze decoration: the design was painted in underglaze cobalt blue, mainly in outline but with some areas of wash, the piece emerging from the kiln as 'blue-and-white'; then it was sent to the enameller for colouring in translucent enamels. The first examples were just in yellow and green, but by the second half of the 1400s yellow, green, aubergine, turquoise and black enamels had been developed. The technique is called *doucai*, meaning 'clashing colours': the contrast between the embedded underglaze design and the colours floating on top gives the decoration a vibrant quality through depth. A number of exquisite *doucai* cups were made during Chenghua's reign, some simple bowl-shaped wine cups (as here), others raised on a foot, probably following a silver prototype.

By the early 18th century such pieces were already highly prized specimens in the Chinese Imperial collection of antique ceramics. The emperor Qianlong (reigned 1735–95), himself a notable antiquarian and scholar, commissioned copies of favourite pieces in the palace collection – from the same kilns that had made the originals 300 years earlier, and that had made copies for Qianlong's immediate predecessor, Yongzheng

*A Chenghua mark and period chicken cup, 1465–87, 7.5 cm (3 in) wide, £2,300,000*

# Kangxi period chicken cup

The Kangxi porcelain is slightly lighter that the Chenghua clay.

The yellow is more of an egg-yolk colour.

The red has a pillar-box tone.

(1723–35) and for the emperor before him, the great Kangxi (1662–1723). Keen to establish 'business as usual' – the Qing emperors had usurped the native Ming Dynasty in 1644 – the new Manchu rulers needed to establish their legitimacy. This in part they did by adopting and espousing traditional Chinese values: not least in ceramics where 'repeats' of old Ming patterns were ordered, the new dynasty making its stamp in the time-honored system of four- and six-character reign marks.

It is rare for unrecorded imperial pieces to appear in the West and a Chenghua 'palace-piece' has yet to turn up on an *Antiques Roadshow*. But in view of the potential sum at stake, a mistaken identification would be disastrous.

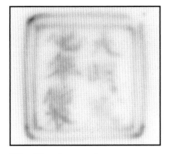

*The Chenghua marks, in underglaze blue, are slightly out of focus due to the oilier glaze used during this period.*

*The Kangxi marks, also in underglaze blue, are much clearer than the earlier examples.*

## Reign marks

From the earliest Ming emperor Hongwu (1368–98) onwards Chinese potters have marked porcelains destined for the emperor with a *nienhao* – a four- or six-character mark incorporating the emperor's name. In a six-character mark the first two characters give the dynasty (either 'Great Ming' or 'Great Qing') while the last two simply read *nien zhou* – 'made in the year'. The important characters, therefore, are the middle pair (bottom right and top left in a two-row mark) giving the emperor's reign name.

The majority of Chinese porcelains reaching the West prior to the late 19th century were generally part of the China Trade. To place the reigning emperor's mark on a piece destined for the Foreign Devils (Europeans) would have been unthinkable. Earlier emperors' marks were therefore used (typically 'Chenghua' under the Kangxi reign) – more out of tact than out of any desire to deceive.

The most obvious difference between the two bowls is in the marks: one bears the mark of Chenghua, the other of Kangxi. But as the vast majority of Chinese porcelains in the West carry marks of emperors much earlier than the period of manufacture, we can only be confident that they are right by comparing the raw material of the two pieces.

*A Kangxi mark and period chicken cup, 1662–1723, 7.5 cm (3 in) wide, £230,000*

# KRAAK

## Chinese kraak

Chinese porcelain arrived in Europe during the Song dynasty (960–1279), but it was a rare and extremely costly object of admiration and awe. So unusual was this material – it was thin, it could be decorated, it did not chip or crack easily, it produced a musical note when struck and, wonder of wonders, it was translucent – that it was mounted in gold and jewels and presented to kings and princes.

It was the Portuguese who began to import Chinese porcelain in quantity in the late 16th and early 17th centuries. In 1603 a trading ship named the *Santa Catarina* was captured by the Dutch and brought back to Amsterdam. There the contents were auctioned, including a huge haul – over 100,000 pieces – of blue-and-white porcelain. The type of vessel was known as a carrack, which was pronounced *kraak* by the Dutch, and the name has now transferred to the porcelain.

The style was to remain popular for about a century, roughly 1550–1650. At the beginning of the 17th century, the ruling dynasty in China, the Ming, who had controlled the empire since 1368, began to totter. They slowly lost ground over about 20 years to the incoming Manchu who were to reign as the Qing from 1644. During this period, known as the Transitional, porcelain was still made in Jingdezhen, but in reduced quantities.

*The dish is thinly potted and moulded with panels. These are distinct on early examples and become less clear the later they get.*

*The rim is nibbled, 'moth-eaten' according to the Japanese.*

*The foot rim has been knife-cut to remove glaze and has kiln grit stuck all round it. The base is pock-marked and where the glaze has missed it has burnt red. Normally, the foot rim is redder than this.*

*The blue at this date is silvery and quite pale, on earlier pieces it was much stronger.*

*There are numerous black and brown holes and pimples in the glaze, which is tight to the body.*

*The painting is sloppy, particularly the scale diaper which is not at all well considered.*

*On handling, it feels lighter than one might expect and also brittle. A knock with a knuckle produces a clear, bright ring.*

*Chinese kraak dish, 1630–50, 35.6 cm (14 in) wide, £600–£1,000*

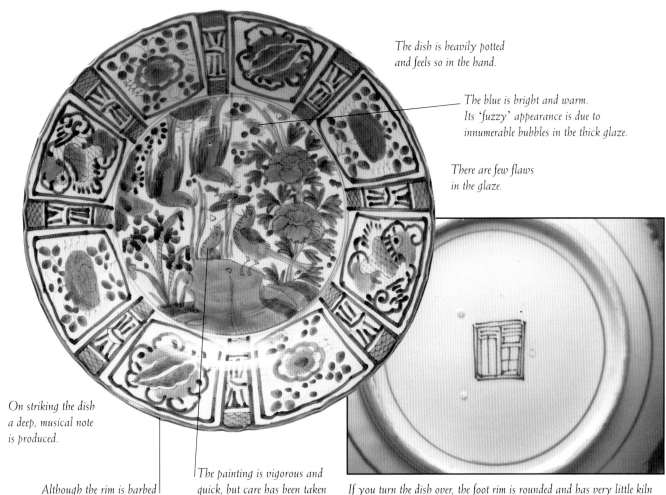

The dish is heavily potted and feels so in the hand.

The blue is bright and warm. Its 'fuzzy' appearance is due to innumerable bubbles in the thick glaze.

There are few flaws in the glaze.

On striking the dish a deep, musical note is produced.

Although the rim is barbed it is not 'nibbled' and the panels are not moulded.

The painting is vigorous and quick, but care has been taken to ensure that the scale diaper 'reads' correctly.

If you turn the dish over, the foot rim is rounded and has very little kiln grit sticking to it. It has burnt redder here than is usual. The base has a single blue line (the Chinese invariably paint two lines, if any). There are three stilt marks on which the piece stood in the kiln. The blue mark in the centre reads fuku (happiness); Japanese kraak frequently bears a mark, often that of the Chinese emperor Chenghua (1465–87). The rim has a flower trail, more in common with earlier Chinese kraak.

## Japanese kraak

The Dutch, by then the dominant trading nation, needed to fill the gap and turned to Japanese manufacturers to supply their European markets. While they ordered new classes of wares, including – for the first time to be seen in Europe – coloured enamels, old favourites such as kraak continued. It is possible that the Dutch gave Dutch delftware copies of kraak as samples for the Japanese to copy; certainly they did this for the Japanese copies of Transitional wares. On the whole, the kraak made at Arita – the main centre of Japanese porcelain production – was better than that made at the end of Chinese production. By the middle of the 17th century, Chinese potting was irregular and the painting was slapdash, some of the motifs, particularly on the back, having degenerated into simple circles.

Japanese kraak, like the Chinese, was for export, not domestic use. Its impact on Japanese porcelain production was dramatic: in 1658 one chest of porcelain went for export, the following year over 65,000 pieces were sent abroad.

*Japanese kraak plate, Sarugawa kiln, c.1680, 35.2 cm (13⅞ in) wide, £1,200–£1,500*

# Persian kraak

Quantities of kraak were imported into Europe, but it was also popular throughout Asia, particularly amongst the Muslims; the Topkapi in Istanbul, for example, has a vast collection. Inevitably, potters in the countries to which kraak was exported tried to undercut the originals in price, or simply fill a gap in the market. Some Persian copies, which are not true porcelain but a type of white faience, are named after the city of Kirman.

These Persian copies, like the Japanese, helped to make up the Chinese shortfall during and after the Ming / Manchu war years. The softer material of Persian faience means that it is very prone to damage; and so examples are now rare.

## Underglaze blue

Underglaze blue, which is cobalt oxide painted onto the raw body before the glaze is applied and the piece fired, is often thought to be a Chinese discovery, but the Persians got there first. In fact, much Chinese cobalt was imported from Persia. Chinese underglaze blue dates from about 1325 and, once established, flourished very rapidly.

*The panels, which usually show precious objects, here display birds and insects among flowers.*

*The rim has a few nibbles.*

*The dish is light in weight and feels 'biscuity'. It has no translucency but the paste is whiter than either the Chinese or Japanese. The blue is very bright and clear. The glaze has minute bubbles leading to a slight fuzziness and is discoloured by brown patches, particularly on the reverse.*

*The foot rim is thin and high and has been ground down. Cracks discolour brown. (The white dots on either side of the crack here are where rivets have been removed.)*

*Curiously, while Chinese kraak is almost unknown with any form of mark, the Persians rated marked wares most highly, and spurious Chinese marks are often found. Shown here is a square mark, which the potter must have hoped would be taken for a Chinese seal.*

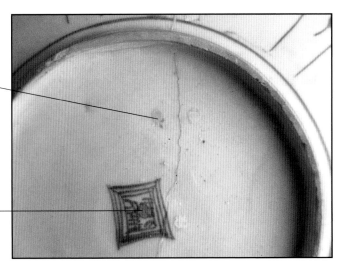

*Persian kraak dish, Kirman, c.1660, 26.2 cm (10¼ in) wide, damaged £300–£500, perfect £1,800–£2,500*

The dish is not translucent.

The panels are not moulded and the rim is not barbed, but some glaze is flaking away exposing the reddish biscuit body.

The blue here is particularly bright and clear, later it becomes inkier. Where there are washes, the blue breaks up into circles of light and dark.

The glaze is smooth and has a few dots exposing the body.

The dish is light for its size and does not usually have a note when struck.

The dot structure of the transfer print can be seen clearly when viewed under a magnifying glass.

The quality of the drawing is poor – this is particularly obvious on the left-hand side of the rock where the water swirls look like a snake.

## Dutch kraak

Dutch, German and English potters all made copies of kraak in tin-glazed earthenware, known as delftware, but they were no match for the porcelain originals in terms of practicality – delftware chips and cracks easily, the glaze flakes, the soft body absorbs water and fat and it is not, of course, translucent.

The Dutch used different coloured clays to try to obtain as white a fired body as possible. To begin with only the front was white tin-glazed, but later the back was also. They also brightened up the decoration by applying *kwaart*, a transparent lead glaze. Unlike the Chinese originals, Dutch kraak is often marked with the manufacturers' initials, symbol or name of the pottery. These were usually taken from the name of the old brewery in which most delftware potteries were working. So ingrained was kraak in Dutch style that pieces were still being made well into the 18th century and a revival took place in the last quarter of the 19th century to cater for the tourist trade.

## Japanese printed 'kraak'

At the end of the 19th century, when collecting Chinese blue-and-white – old Nanking as it was called – was at fever pitch, a manufactory in (probably) Japan produced a range of deceptive transfer-printed dishes and plates in kraak style. The patterns of the dishes were re-drawn by the factory, as photographing an original would have produced distortion. The result usually loses something of the original. Be suspicious if the porcelain or earthenware surface is very smooth.

*Dutch kraak dish, late 17th century,*
*33 cm (13 in) wide, £500–£1,200*

*Japanese transfer-printed kraak dish,*
*c.1900, 35 cm (13¾ in) wide, £100–£150*

# IMARI VASES

*The knops are, like the 20th-century vases (right), in the form of* shi-shi *(Buddhist lions).*

*The hand-painted design has an unmistakable fluidity about it.*

*The shape of the vase is typical of the late 17th and early 18th centuries.*

*There is plenty of space round the design.*

In the second half of the 17th century, wars in China (*see* kraak *page 22*) saw the sacking of Jingdezhen where most Chinese porcelain was made. The Dutch, who were the principle traders, sought a new source – Japan. While the Japanese have a long ceramics tradition, porcelain was relatively new and the Dutch had to guide the potters at Arita, the main centre in Japan, as to their needs. From there came the famous Kakiemon wares, as did the popular Imari style.

Japan had, in the 16th century, welcomed foreigners to her shores. These were mainly the Spanish and Portuguese whose priests immediately began converting the natives. This was tolerated, but when fighting began between the sects, the Shogun threw out all foreigners. The only traders allowed to continue were the Dutch and Chinese, who had to be content with a reclaimed mudflat, Deshima Island, in Nagasaki Harbour. Their wares, with their distinctive strong palette of underglaze blue, iron-red and gilding, were named after the port of transhipment: Imari.

Imari was hugely popular in Holland and houses were designed with enormous fireplaces around which the garnitures (sets of vases, usually three, five or seven) could be displayed. Mary, who married William of Orange in 1677, brought the style to England. They ruled as William and Mary from 1689 to 1694, when Mary died.

There is a curious gap in our knowledge of what was being made in Japan between about 1750 and 1850 when, in 1853, the Americans broke the isolationist policy of the Shogun and the supremacy of the emperor began its fight back. Shortly after this, wares began to be made for the West which, by the end of the 19th century, had become a flood. One of the popular designs on Imari ware (although examples are by no means

*Pair of genuine Imari vases, late 17th or early 18th century, 61 cm (24 in) tall, £6,000–£8,000*

# Fake Imari vases

*If you look at the pattern with an eye glass you will be able to see a basic black transfer print.*

*These vases purport to date from the late 17th or early 18th century, but the Black Ship design did not emerge until the 19th century.*

*The design is much denser and more rigid than the genuine example.*

*The use of European coat of arms would dramatically increase the value if this was real.*

common) was of the European 'black' trading ships. Unlike most export wares these were also popular in Japan. The pattern was, however, restricted to bowls and dishes.

About 15 years ago a class of porcelain made in the Far East – in both Canton and Taiwan – began to appear on the market. It flooded into home interiors shops and then made its way onto the secondary market – antique fairs, markets and so on. In the beginning, the wares made were quite deceptive, but quality has dropped of late, as has the price. They are rarely exact copies of earlier wares, more often they are in-the-style-of. What is important to remember is that the originals were always hand-painted throughout, the copies have a basic transfer print in black for the painter to use as a guide. This can be seen with a hand lens or even with the naked eye. Another giveaway is that very many large vases and bowls have red or brown mud smeared inside the covers or, most commonly, on the base. Any such appearance should immediately act as a warning.

*Pair of imitation Imari vases, Chinese, c.1980, 58.5 cm (23 in) tall, about £400*

## The clarity of colours

Underglaze blue in 17th-century Japanese porcelain appears 'fuzzy' because the colour is filtered through millions of tiny bubbles in the very thick glaze. The blue is also a slatey colour, unlike the blue on 19th-century pieces, which is usually bright and clear. The red enamel is applied over the glaze and therefore remains crisp.

# FAMILLE ROSE TOBACCO-LEAF JUG

One of the few ceramic techniques to have made its way from the West to the East rather than the other way round is a palette known as *famille rose*. The pink was brought to China by the Jesuits late in the reign of Emperor Kangxi (1662–1723) and examples can be found on porcelain from 1720. The previously rather restricted palette now included a wide range of colours, often mixed with white to provide opaque tones. Very shortly afterwards *famille rose*, originally only on pieces made for the emperor and court use, appeared on export wares.

During the reign of Emperor Qianlong (1735–95) a vast number of different patterns were exported to the West, among them the tobacco-leaf and pseudo-tobacco-leaf designs. Rather than the more usual sprigs or sprays of flowers, here the flowers and leaves spread over most of the available space. The name tobacco-leaf is itself somewhat dubious as the leaves are more likely derived from tropical foliage. The flower is not that of the tobacco, but looks like a cross between a passion flower and a peony. The related pseudo-tobacco-leaf pattern is even further from its name. The design remained popular into the 19th century. It would have been ordered by the supercargo, the representative of the East India Company who negotiated with the Canton decorators. They painted the coloured designs onto the Jingdezhen-made blanks. Co-operation was needed between the two centres as the blue leaves on the originals were in underglaze blue and were painted and glazed in Jingdezhen, leaving the rest to be filled in in Canton.

The body has a distinct bluish tinge.

There is great freedom and fluidity in the painting.

As with all old porcelain, a magnifying glass will reveal hundreds of minute scratches in the glaze and, most particularly, in the gold which may be very rubbed.

The porcelain has small black spots in the glaze to which there is an element of 'wobbliness'.

The rim is not gilt.

The flowers have plenty of white space around them.

The leaves and flowers are not outlined in black.

The foot rim is burnt deep orange.

*Original* famille rose *tobacco-leaf jug,*
C.1770, £2,000–£3,000

# Modern copies

Very good copies of the *famille rose* tobacco-leaf pattern have been made for about 15 years in Portugal, more are now being made in the East and are available from perfectly legitimate sources such as interior design and porcelain shops and chain stores. They are reasonably good value and very decorative. The problem arises when they escape from these sources on to the 'antique' market – fairs, shops and centres. They are, however, fairly easy to identify.

*The decoration follows the originals, but is very stiff and lacks the freedom of the originals. The colours are hand-applied over a black transfer and include colours never found on 18th-century pieces, such as the dove-grey that replaces the pale blue. Enamels are either too shiny or have an unusual rough, bubbly finish, feeling like sandpaper. The dark blue here is in solid overglaze enamel, whereas on the original the blue was underglaze and with variations in tone. There are no scratches in the glaze, but watch for false wear applied with sandpaper.*

*Enamel colours are standing proud of the black lines and are easily felt as raised above the level of the porcelain. The usual Chinese gold (which tends to a thin rich / brassy gold colour) is here replaced, including on the rim, by a curious, matt metallic orange.*

*There is less white space around this spray of flowers than on the original.*

*The transfer-printed, matt-black outline is either solid or breaking up.*

*The surface is heavily potted in a fault-free, shiny-glazed white porcelain that is opaque.*

*Copies are mostly bowls in two sizes, although these are very rare in original services.*

*The base bears the four-character mark of the emperor, but in the wrong order: nianzhi Qianlong. Normally it would read ta Qing Qianlong nianzhi (made in the reign of the great Qing emperor Qianlong). The mark is transfer-printed in red, which was never the case in the 18th century; additionally, export wares were not marked. This example also has a number 56 (probably a size or pattern number) in barely visible white enamel. A European number always denotes a 20th-century piece.*

*The foot rim has only a very faint orange tinge.*

*Copy of* famille rose *tobacco-leaf bowl, late 20th century, £14*

# A CHINESE EXPORT 'SCOTSMAN' PLATE

The East India Companies that traded with China were strictly controlled. In the English Company, all the blue-and-white porcelain – the bulk of what was carried – was bought in Canton by the supercargo to written demands from London. When this was landed after the return voyage, it was auctioned. The enamelled (coloured) wares were under the control of the supercargo who, along with the rest of the crew, was allowed to trade privately. Again, this was tightly supervised and the number of boxes per crew member was strictly allocated. Once in London, these too had to be auctioned and the crew member was often in the curious position of having to buy his own property! He did, of course, receive the proceeds minus a commission taken by the company.

Just as today, fashion was fickle and the traders were always trying to find designs that would tempt the market, often reflecting up-to-the-minute events. Sometime before 1745 a plate was ordered to commemorate the shooting at the Tower of London of Rifleman Shaw of the 42nd Regiment, and the sending of Piper Macdonnel (or Macdonald) to Georgia as a convict for treason. These two soldiers were part of a Jacobite mutiny. The Chinese were given engravings of the soldiers dating from 1743 by George Bickham after paintings by John Bowles. The two figures were combined onto the one plate, the piper being reversed so that they both look inwards.

The copy is probably the work of the 'Milanese forger' who produced a string of dud Chinese export wares in the 1980s. He was extremely talented and it is no wonder that the copies fooled many people including leading collectors, dealers and auctioneers at the time. One of these copies (of which there about 20 known examples) has the seal mark of the Emperor Qianlong on the back – an unknown feature and a good example of a faker or forger over-egging the custard.

Often one needs to examine every small element of a piece to be sure of its genuineness or otherwise. All the points listed below are minor slips which, taken individually, would probably be overlooked and not enough to condemn the copy.

The most obvious difference between an original Chinese export 'Scotsman' plate and a European fake is that the latter fails to capture the oriental style of painting. For instance, a Chinese-painted figure of the piper should be somewhat squat with dumpy legs, while that in the fake opposite has longer, almost balletic legs. The figures fill less space than on the original – an unusual feature as it is common on fakes and forgeries for there to be less white porcelain showing. The soldier's fingers and eyes should also look particularly eastern if the plate is a genuine example.

The original palette is much lighter; Rifleman Shaw's jacket is bright red on the Chinese example, while the piper's jacket is greyish in tone. In the plate opposite the jackets are maroon and deep black respectively.

You should also look carefully at the scenes in the side panels. Chinese-drawn trees typically have multi-angled branches, while those opposite are much smoother. Also, the birds themselves are much less detailed.

If you look at the colour of the plate opposite, there is an overall black/grey sanding of the background under a very thin glaze. This is quite atypical of Chinese porcelain of the period which, while it may contain the odd black imperfection, does not display an overall 'smoking'. This has been caused by having to strip the original decoration, probably *famille rose* flowers, and then either to re-glaze or, more likely, simply refire the plate. Whichever method was chosen it has resulted in a 'dry', imperfect surface.

# Fake 'Scotsman' Plate

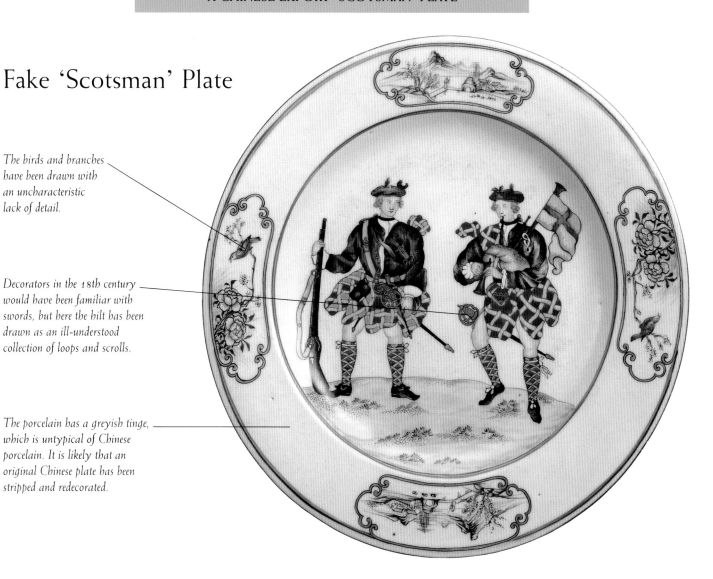

*The birds and branches have been drawn with an uncharacteristic lack of detail.*

*Decorators in the 18th century would have been familiar with swords, but here the hilt has been drawn as an ill-understood collection of loops and scrolls.*

*The porcelain has a greyish tinge, which is untypical of Chinese porcelain. It is likely that an original Chinese plate has been stripped and redecorated.*

*The Chinese were not used to drawing European eyes, and so usually gave them an oriental slant. Here, however, the eyes are convincingly Western-looking.*

*The hands here look quite realistic, while on the Chinese originals they look like the fruit Buddha's finger-citron.*

*The original kilt, as drawn by a Chinese, was poorly understood. Even on this forgery the pleats look like tartan haggises*

*A 'Chinese export plate' possibly by the 'Milanese forger', 1980s, £60–£80*

# A MAIOLICA PLATE

Maiolica plates were often on mythological themes, such as this image of Pan with Venus and Cupid.

*The foreground bank is eroded with fissures, cracks and crevices crumbling in detail.*

During the 19th century, one of the most popular souvenirs brought back from Italy by wealthy collectors on the Grand Tour were the brightly coloured, tin-glazed earthenware dishes, vases and sculptures known as 'maiolica'. During the Italian High Renaissance of the 16th century, the foremost maiolica-producing centres were Venice, Tuscany and Umbria. Particularly sought after were the brightly coloured dishes of the Urbino, Deruta and Gubbio workshops. Some pieces were considered on a par with the works of Raphael (who was erroneously believed to have painted maiolica 'Raphael ware').

Subject matter was usually mythological (the Fall of Troy, Perseus freeing Andromeda, a scene from Ovid) or religious (St Francis receiving the stigmata) and such story-telling or *istoriato* scenes were almost always copied from available prints of the day. Particularly fine pieces might incorporate the shield or crest of a noble family suspended within the design. Titles were inscribed on the reverse, sometimes with a date and occasionally the mark of a workshop.

The maiolica tondo illustrated opposite depicts The Holy Mother and Child. Behind them stands Joseph and in the foreground is a monkey. The dish has a distinguished recent history: it was the subject of a 1930 article in *Burlington* magazine; it featured in the Italian Exhibition of 1930; it passed through Christie's in 1936 and it entered both the Courtauld and Oppenheimer collections. But despite all this exposure, it is a forgery.

Elements from at least three separate Dürer prints have been employed in the composition. *The Virgin and Child with a Monkey* (circa 1498) gives us the three foreground figures – but the Holy Infant's attention has been switched from the bird on his hand (much wizened from the original finch) to the figure standing behind them, hat in hand. This seems to be St James, lifted from *The*

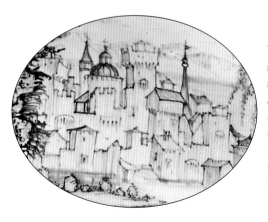

*The Cafaggiolo workshop was situated in the grounds of the Medici villa, north of Florence. Run at first by two brothers, Stefan and Piero di Filippo, its mark was a monogram, 'SP'.*

*A Cafaggiolo dish,* c.1510,
£40,000–£60,000

*Virgin Worshipped by Angels and Saints*, one of Dürer's 17 cuts from the *Life of the Virgin*, (circa 1511). Meanwhile, a substantial part of the left-hand side architectural background of receding arches is taken from *The Adoration of the Magi*, another Dürer print from the same series. True, maiolica painters did derive very many of their compositions from prints, but to merge so many prints into one image is very suspicious.

Could the forgery have been exposed without a knowledge of the works of Dürer? The forger chose colours that closely correspond to those used at Urbino and Cafaggiolo in the 1520–40 period, including a ruby lustre pigment employed at both Deruta and Cafaggiolo, and only rediscovered in the 1850s. But if we look closely at the ground white, we see a fine mesh of hairline cracks, not normally seen in early 16th-century maiolica. If there were any lingering doubts, a small sample of clay drilled from an unobtrusive part of the foot rim interior would, under a thermoluminescence test (*see page 177*), reveal just how many years ago the clay was last fired.

The dish is now attributed to Ferrucio Mengaroni (1875–1925), whose workshop was situated in Pesaro, 20 miles south of Rimini on the Adriatic coast, not far from Urbino. By the late 1920s several Mengaroni pieces had already been debunked after entering the Victoria & Albert Museum in London. Even so, many of his excellent forgeries still lurk unrecognized in distinguished museums and collections throughout the world.

# Fake by Mengaroni

*Based on several elements from different Dürer prints, this forgery quickly gained credence, catering for both the maiolica and Old Master tastes of the Victorian collector.*

*When compared to the original prints, all the skittish detail of Dürer (the originally random arrangement of stone blocks, now regular) has been smoothed out, while arches are clumsy, halos are not circular and Joseph's hat is messy.*

*The cutaway bank lacks any fine detail.*

*A maiolica dish in the Cafaggiolo/Urbino style, attributed to Ferrucio Mengaroni (1875–1925), £500–£1,000*

# MEISSEN FIGURE OF AVVOCATO

*This example is in a restrained palette; very often they are in much stronger colours.*

*The eyes are very carefully delineated.*

*The creases in the coat are extremely well defined, as are the flower-form buttons.*

*The flowers on the base, while crisply modelled, are not sharp enough to cut the hand, as is common on many Samson copies.*

The Meissen factory, founded by Augustus the Strong, Elector of Saxony and King of Poland in 1710, produced figures from early on. Augustus, who was a porcelain fanatic, employed some of the greatest ceramic artists of all time to work as painters or modellers. The best known of the latter was Johann Joachim Kändler. He joined the factory in 1733, the year Augustus died, and he, better than anyone before or since, realized the potential of clay for small-scale figures.

It was common in those days for the dining table to be set with spun-sugar figures, often of topical interest, and Kändler began a series of models of figures of court life and from the Italian Comedy – the *Commedia dell'Arte* – including the famous harlequins. These were introduced in 1738 and were completed by 1744. Peter Reinicke, another talented modeller, joined Meissen in 1743, and also contributed to the Comedy series. One of the characters was Avvocato, the lawyer, and is arguably one of the best of the series. In Victorian times, when there was avid collecting of most early porcelain, the Italian Comedy was highly sought after.

One of the best copyists of early ceramics was Samson of Paris, founded by Edme Samson in 1845. He introduced a wide range of reproductions of porcelain, earthenware, enamels, glass and so on which cause so much trouble today. The factory was inherited by his more famous son Emile and huge numbers of

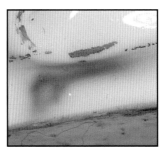

*The Meissen mark is painted on the back of the figure near the base rather than on the underside, as was common later. The blue has run under the glaze, so that the mark is small and ill-defined. In the 1740s bases were flat and were sometimes ground flatter on a wheel if they warped in the kiln.*

*Genuine Meissen figure of Avvocato, c.1740, 18 cm (7¼ in) tall, £6,000–£8,000*

reproductions were made by him and by his son and grandson, right up until the 1960s. The factory, certainly early on, marked all the wares that it produced with its own series of marks so that they could not be mistaken for the real thing. We cannot be sure, but it is likely that towards the end of the period, unmarked, and therefore more deceptive, pieces were being made. When Samson marked his copies of Meissen he did so with a simple cross, crossed by a single line in the centre; close, but not exactly copying the Meissen crossed swords. He also frequently impressed his own model numbers from type into the base.

Traditionally, almost every copy of any earlier porcelain whether English, Continental or Chinese has been lumped together as 'Samson'. It is quite clear that there were other manufacturers in Paris, including Paul Bocquillon, who made copies, but we are unable now to know who made what. When it comes to English porcelain, these copies are easily exposed as they are in hard-paste rather than soft-paste porcelain. The position is much more difficult when it comes to oriental and, most particularly, Meissen porcelain. The Samson paste is very close to that of Meissen in both its colour and glazing and the enamels are very little different. Quite often Samson fell into the typical 19th-century trap of 'prettifying' his faces, which in the originals were often rather grotesque. The original 18th-century figures often (but not here) display grins and a mouthful of teeth. This is uncommon in the 19th century. The eyes of 18th-century figures are, with a very few exceptions, never blue.

# Samson figure of Avvocato

*This Samson Avvocato is very close to the Meissen in the typical exaggerated pose, the paste and the modelling. However, the flowerheads on the robe are much less well defined and are painted in a red which would not have been used in the 1740s.*

*Normally, the yellow would be much more a yolk, rather than a lemon, hue.*

*The reverse of the Samson copy showing where the Samson cross mark has been ground away at the foot to make it easier to pass the figure off as genuine Meissen. Any piece of porcelain with a ground-off patch should be treated with suspicion.*

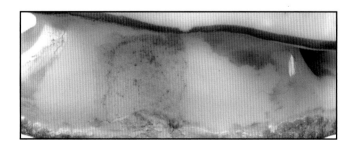

*Imitation Meissen figure of Avvocato, 13.3 cm (5¼ in) tall, £200–£300*

# HEROLD-DECORATED MEISSEN PORCELAIN

*The amount of white space left undecorated on this coffee pot gives it a great sense of airiness.*

*The coffee pot is cracked, and the gilding has been rubbed in places, suggesting that it has been used rather than kept in a cabinet.*

*The chinoiserie design is after the master J. G. Herold.*

The Meissen factory (*see also page 34*) employed some superb painters. As the West was familiar with porcelain from both China and Japan, it was their styles, filtered through Western eyes, that Meissen copied. The East – Cathay – was where porcelain came from, along with other luxury goods such as lacquer, silks and tea. Chinoiserie, that wonderful amalgam of East and West, had first appeared in the 17th century and reappeared, mixed with the Baroque at the end of that century.

The earliest Meissen wares were red stoneware, followed by creamy-white teabowls and vases. Before long, enamels were being used in Japanese Kakiemon or Chinese style. These were introduced by the famous Johann Gregor Herold (or Höroldt) who joined Meissen from Vienna in 1720. He was also responsible for a wide range of new enamel colours. He drew a number of sketches that were used as models by the Meissen painters and any attribution to the hand of Herold is subject to much debate. His designs were reproduced in the *Shultz Codex*, published in 1978, and any such source material is ideal for anyone trying to make a copy.

It has been said that the porcelain expert learns 200 shades of white and, while an exaggeration, there is some truth in it. What the expert looks at before he or she gets involved with the decoration, gilding or form is the exact colour of the porcelain 'body' or 'paste'. Most factories experimented with different ingredients producing colour changes in the body, tiny nuances of hue that can be learnt. It is now almost impossible to recreate any European porcelain body with enough conviction to fool the expert eye. The faker has to turn to other means. Most common is 'stripping' or 'skimming', where the original decoration is removed from a genuine piece by either grinding on a wheel or etching off with hydrofluoric acid.

*Genuine Meissen silver-mounted coffee pot, painted in the manner of J. G. Herold, c.1725, 18 cm (7 in) tall, £5,200*

# Redecorated Meissen plate

*The strange pink on the border under the gilding is known as Böttger lustre. It has been simulated rather well here.*

*The decoration is after a design that appeared in the* Schultz Codex.

*The faker has been over-enthusiastic with the decoration (probably in the hope of making the plate seem to be a highly important example). The amount of white left is uncharacteristic of the period.*

The resultant blank can then be redecorated with a more expensive design. The most common factory to suffer this indignity is Sèvres (*see page 38*), but it occasionally happens to Meissen. The plate above was originally decorated with flowers and leaves and would have been fairly cheap – about £20 – when it was stripped. A pair to this redecorated plate passed undetected through a London saleroom for £19,000!

This plate started out life in Meissen in about 1740–50. It is therefore of the right material and bears the Meissen crossed swords in underglaze blue, although these are in a later style than would have been appropriate for the decoration. The design is so elaborate that it should immediately put you on guard. It is not known when this copy was done, certainly it is post-war and possibly after the publication of the *Shultz Codex* (its design is based on one from the *Codex*). It is one of the most convincing fakes to come to attention.

*Meissen plate, 1740–50, stripped and redecorated mid-20th century, £100*

## Scratching

If the plate is photographed under extreme raking light, an extraordinary amount of scratching is revealed. While this might be expected on a dinner plate (as this piece started out in life) it would be highly unlikely on a cabinet or dessert plate. Furthermore, the scratches are under the enamel, which means that the plate must have been scratched before decoration. A scratch in glaze or enamel leaves a ragged edge, which is readily visible under a lens. Here the edges are smooth, because the plate has been refired. Visible here also is the ghost of a leaf – the slightly frosted foliage is revealed where the acid has bitten in to the porcelain. Many redecorated pieces, if held in such a raking light, can be thus exposed.

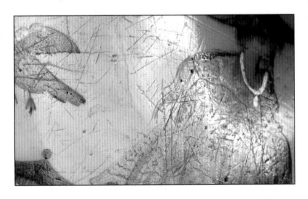

# SÈVRES JEWELLED CUP AND SAUCER

The Sèvres factory was founded by Louis XV in 1745. Augustus the Strong, King of Poland and Elector of Saxony, had set up the Meissen factory, and Louis, who considered himself the most important person in the world, was not going to be outdone by an upstart from Germany. In his warrant to Elois Brichard and Charles Adam he stated that he wanted them to make 'porcelain in the style of Saxony, painted and gilded and depicting human figures'. In other words, they were to copy Meissen, making both wares and figures. The actual secret of making true or hard-paste porcelain eluded them until 1769, and it can be argued with some conviction that the glory of Sèvres lies in its soft-paste wares.

Louis spent large sums of money on the factory, in order for it to achieve the highest standards; in fact he became the sole owner of Sèvres in 1759. There was a constant drive to achieve beautiful pieces in new styles and new colours. First of these was *bleu céleste* in 1753, which was followed by *bleu nouveau* in 1763 (later named *beau bleu*) and the famous *rose* (rose Pompadour in England). This final design was named after Mme de Pompadour, the mistress of Louis XV, who loved porcelain and who had enormous influence over the factory.

Sèvres continued to initiate new styles and forms under Louis XVI. One of these was the so-called jewelled ware, which was a favourite of Marie Antoinette. Jewelling was developed by

*The rich, deep blue ground (bleu nouveau) is without faults, and the white enamel is very white.*

*The gilding has been burnished after firing and then tooled to produce patterns, which catch the light.*

*The enamelling is highly translucent, so that the tooling of the gold shows through from beneath.*

*Some of the gold and enamelling are missing, which is almost inevitable in pieces of this age.*

*The pattern is superbly balanced and executed, and the decoration, while rich, has a restraint to it rarely found in copies.*

*Genuine Sèvres cup and saucer (goblet litron et soucoupe), 1784, cup 6.6 cm (2⅝ in), £4,000–£6,000*

Joseph Coteau and Philippe Parpette and was in production for about 10 years from 1776. It was a complex process (despite Parpette claiming that nothing could be simpler) and involved the production of steel dies, which were used to cut tiny pieces of gold foil. These were then engraved with patterns and had either white (to imitate pearls) or translucent enamels dropped on them. The foils were fired and then attached to the piece of porcelain with enamel and fired again. The process was hugely difficult – especially because the enamelled foils were prone to drop off in the kiln or later – and was always expensive, largely due to the amount of gold used. The delicacy of the pieces meant that they were never really meant for use but were intended for the cabinet.

The overall effect of the jewelling was one of extreme richness, quality and craftsmanship, all attributes much admired in the 19th century. The Victorians made quantities of copies of jewelled pieces, often on Sèvres blanks that had been sold off after the Revolution. Most of the copies have decoration dating from the 1860s and 1870s. One of the reasons so many were made is the high prices paid for jewelled wares from the 19th century to World War II. Post-war the style fell from favour, although taste is now changing again.

*Paintings of historical figures on genuine Sèvres are almost unheard of (doubt any piece you see), but are common on copies.*

*This rose pink was the favourite colour of Mme de Pompadour, and was never made again after her death in 1764. As the jewelled technique was not developed until over 10 years later, this pair could not possibly be genuine. Also, the colour of the pink is far too weak.*

*There are too few jewelled dots and too much gilding, covering a higher proportion of the ground, for this set to be genuine.*

## Spit-back

A fired piece of soft-paste porcelain will absorb moisture through the foot rim. When the piece has added decoration and is re-fired, this moisture has to escape; most re-exits through the foot rim, but some will escape through the glaze. Often, as here, it is in a ring of minute black or brown volcanoes round the centre of the base, which is known as spit-back. It may appear anywhere and often takes the form of a cloud of pin-prick black dots. Any appearance should act as a warning, although it can appear on genuine pieces.

*Reproduction Sèvres jewelled cup and saucer, French, c.1865, cup 7 cm (2¾ in), £300–£400*

# VIENNA PORCELAIN

*Hand-painted enamels should reveal occasional brushstrokes, and single colours should vary in tone within the work.*

*Look for the density of colour, both in the central panel and in the compartmentalized borders.*

Like the frequently copied crossed swords of the Meissen factory (*see pages 34–7*), the famous shield mark of the Vienna factory is likely to lead unsuspecting collectors astray. Of the hundreds of Vienna-marked porcelains brought along to the *Antiques Roadshow*, only a fraction were made and decorated at the Imperial factory between the 18th and mid-19th centuries. A much larger group of pieces, while actually made at the factory, were sold as blanks when it closed in 1864. The pieces were pre-marked in underglaze blue, and were sometimes impressed with date-code numerals. Such perfectly genuine Vienna porcelains give the impression of having been factory decorated, but the painting may have been done years later.

The only way to identify a later decorated piece of Vienna porcelain is to analyze the quality of the painting and decide whether it is good enough for the Imperial factory. To do this you will need to examine a number of genuine pieces from auction houses or museums. Check that any painted human faces look 'right' for the period. The colour and quality of the gilding is also revealing. It should be rich and golden, not thin and brassy.

Fakes are easier to spot. If a piece is earthenware, rather than porcelain, it is not Vienna. If the blue shield is on the glaze, not under it, the mark is wrong. And if the decoration is a print, then the piece cannot be genuine.

## Vienna marks

Dozens of workshops in Austria, Germany and Paris used the underglaze shield mark of Vienna. In addition to the shield, numerals impressed in the clay are a good sign.

*Genuine Viennese vase, C.1860, £3,000–£5,000*

# A question of quality

This vase is Viennese in style, but the printed design is flat and dry in tone, the gilding appears to be stamped with repeated elements, and the overall impression is of a lack of quality.

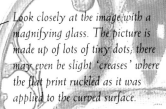

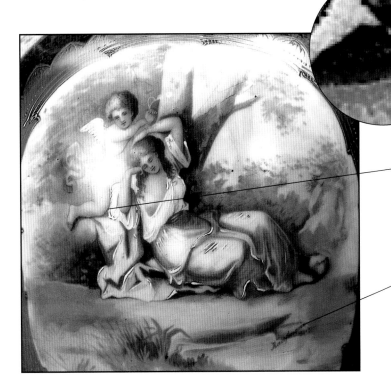

*Look closely at the image with a magnifying glass. The picture is made up of lots of tiny dots; there may even be slight 'creases' where the flat print ruckled as it was applied to the curved surface.*

*Check for a hard, unvaried outline in black or pink – sometimes the outline is printed in its entirety.*

*If the piece is signed by a well-known master, such as Boucher, Fragonard or (as here) Angelica Kauffmann, the piece is much later and invariably printed. As a painter on canvas, Kauffmann is famous for her Classical themes. She never painted on porcelain.*

## Transfer printing

Transfer printing revolutionized ceramic decoration, allowing patterns to be mass-produced in Europe, where potters had previously been competing with hand-painted production-line porcelains from China. Printing techniques reflected ordinary printing on paper processes, from single colour outlines with cross-hatched shading to colour stencils and the later chromolithographs of the late 19th century. Earlier prints in underglaze blue can be hard to identify, as the cobalt would often 'run' during glaze firing, giving a semblance of a hand-drawn line. Later all-over blue printing on earthenware is usually too detailed and 'grainy' to have been done by hand. Late 19th-century full-colour prints are often betrayed by tears or overlaps in the print where it has been laid on. A print may be disguised by free-hand shading to distract the eye from an edge. If in any doubt, use a magnifying glass and look for tell-tale dots.

*Imitation Vienna vase*, c. 1900,
£100–£200

# TOFT SLIPWARE DISH

To a prospector of Early English Pottery the name of 'Toft' is gold. The discovery of an unrecorded 17th-century dish potted in the characteristic red earthenware of Staffordshire, decorated with a mermaid combing her hair, a pelican feeding its young or perhaps a royal family 'tree' of portraits – all trailed and finely dotted in several colours of 'slip', is the ambition not only of any devotee of British ceramics, but also of any general (and wealthy) collector furnishing an interior in the style of Restoration England. Such pieces are eagerly sought after both in England and the

United States, and since there are all too few originals (many pieces being in museums) when they appear at auction prices are high, stimulating the desire to make convincing fakes.

From the mid-17th century onwards, the Toft family – Thomas, Ralph, James and Charles – supplied magnificent slipware dishes that were decorated in a cake-icing technique known as slip-trailing (or tube-lining). Their wares, even if broken and stuck back together again, are today worth tens of thousands of pounds. In many of the finest examples, and for the first time in all English ceramics, the potter's name is displayed in full as part of the overall decorative scheme, showing the high regard with which they held their own work.

'Slip' is the name given to ordinary earthenware clay which is mixed with sufficient water to make

*Slipware should have a lustrous honey glow once fired.*

*The robust border is cross-hatched pale on dark chocolate-brown lines. Although simple, the design is tight, angular and contained.*

*This crack only slightly reduces the value of the dish.*

## Ozzie

Everyone remembers The Owl, one of the *Roadshow*'s most celebrated discoveries. Until Henry Sandon calmly told the innocent owner that her 23-cm (9-in) high quizzical bird with detachable head was a rare and valuable example of Staffordshire slipware, *circa* 1700, Ozzie (as he became known) had perched (headless) on the window sill, serving as a vase rather than as a drinking vessel, his original function. After her 1989 meeting with Henry, the owner feared for the owl's safety and decided to turn her ceramic nest-egg into cash. When the story broke, the Staffordshire bird fetching just under £20,000 at auction (30 years earlier, in 1966, a similar owl fetched £1,050), a whole roost of owls swooped down from people's attics, some old, some not. At this price-level primitive owls are well worth faking.

*Original slipware dish by Thomas Toft, late 17th century, 43 cm (17 in), £30,000–£50,000*

it liquid. In the Staffordshire region clay slips were bleached or tinted (with metallic oxides) to 'earth' colours ranging from pale cream to dark brown. While the very liquid slip was used for dunking an object to cover its dark red body the thicker paste-like slips could be squirted through tubes in lines or dots onto a surface giving a cellular outline. Thus complex patterns and images could be built up. When all the decoration was done the piece was then 'sealed' in a solution of transparent lead glaze, giving the whole piece a honey glow.

## Fake Toft slipware dish

### Aging

The faker tries to create 'oldness' by simulating naïvety and clumsiness: an artificial firing crack has been deliberately scored into the glaze, and the pattern is self-consciously child-like or 'primitive'. In fact, the Tofts produced well-potted and well-glazed pieces.

*The border is executed in only one colour, its spacing is irregular and it fails to stay within the exact flange of the rim.*

*The studied informality of the name and date inscription has been done with a knowledge of 17th-century lettering, but has been placed completely off balance to the design.*

*Fake slipware dish inscribed 'Ralph Toft, 1676', but c.1980, 46 cm (18 in), £100–£200*

# CHELSEA RABBIT TUREEN

A vast proportion of the porcelain nymphs and shepherds brought to the average auction-house or the *Antiques Roadshow* bear a gold or red anchor mark, purporting to be from the illustrious 18th-century English porcelain factory, Chelsea. But 99.9 per cent of these figures are copies – usually from France or Germany – recognizable as such because they have a hard, greyish, flinty white body, whereas Chelsea is always soft.

Chelsea was the aristocrat of early English porcelain factories, often making complex (and therefore very expensive) shapes and forms. Its figures, vases and tableware were amongst the most desirable china commodities, from the very first years of manufacture in the 1740s. A major wave of 'china mania' rose in the 1860s when avid collectors, such as Lady Charlotte Schreiber, drove prices through the roof, and from then on it became worthwhile to produce Chelsea copies.

Amongst the most accomplished factories for making copies was the Paris factory of Samson. Founded in 1845, the Samson factory developed copyists' skills in porcelain and earthenware, initially by making replacements for damaged or disfigured 18th-century dinner services as well

as straightforward reproductions for museums and collectors. It was an easy step from the manufacture of substitutes to the unsolicited making of pieces in a certain style. And Samson made everything. So prolific and technically competent are the Samson creations that there has been a tendency to attribute any convincing fake to this factory. In many cases the pieces are marked with underglaze-blue crossed lines (sometimes difficult to distinguish from Meissen crossed swords), a distinctive double 'S' motif or a square iron-red 'chop' mark resembling a Chinese seal and usually reserved for oriental imitations. Where a piece is thus marked, we can be sure of the factory. But if a piece is unmarked, or if a mark has been erased (*see page 35*) proceed with caution.

When deciding whether a piece of porcelain is Chelsea, you need to establish that it is soft-paste. If it is, the porcelain will be creamy-white, and the enamel colours will have sunk or merged into the surface during firing. If the piece is chipped, the exposed fracture surface will appear granular and porous – like a sugar cube.

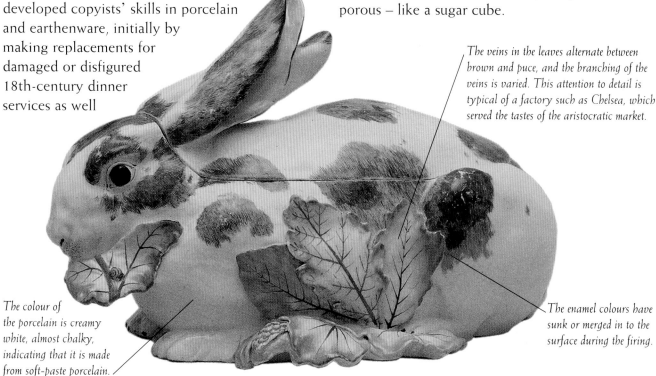

*The veins in the leaves alternate between brown and puce, and the branching of the veins is varied. This attention to detail is typical of a factory such as Chelsea, which served the tastes of the aristocratic market.*

*The colour of the porcelain is creamy white, almost chalky, indicating that it is made from soft-paste porcelain.*

*The enamel colours have sunk or merged in to the surface during the firing.*

*Genuine Chelsea porcelain tureen, c.1752–56, 26 cm (10 in) long, £20,000–£40,000*

## Hard- or soft-paste?

'Paste' is a term used to describe the clay from which a ceramic object is fashioned. A porcelain body is either 'hard-' or 'soft-paste', depending on the actual ingredients used. Learning how to tell the difference between hard and soft can take years of practice and daily handling, but this skill is important in determining an origin, particularly where the difference between a fake and a genuine article can be decided simply on the basis of hard or soft clay.

*On the base of the tureen, just behind the rabbit's tail, are two S's crossed – the mark of Samson!*

*This rabbit has a flinty, glassy look. The white is not creamy but very slightly grey.* ————————

# Samson rabbit tureen

The colour of the porcelain is a giveaway when deciding whether the rabbit tureen below is a Chelsea original or a Samson copy – it has a flinty, 'glassy' look that is typical of hard-paste. The lack of detail in the decoration should also make you suspicious. It always pays to look carefully for a mark, even on an unglazed biscuit surface, and the base of this tureen bears the mark of Samson. Perhaps even this mark, easily copied, will one day be faked, as Samson becomes a collectable factory in its own right.

We are lucky to have two examples side-by-side: it is easy to distinguish differences. But it is a rare luxury for a collector to have a 'rightun' (or a 'wrongun') available for such direct comparison. Besides, with so many English porcelains, all with a number of different ceramic recipes and each copying the successful designs of the other, we cannot on the above observations alone rule out other 18th-century contemporaries before opting for a copyist such as Samson. To become expert you have to build up a memory of comparisons, mentally filing the relevant attributes with your own words, just as a wine expert learns distinctive shades of red and uses a personal vocabulary to store characteristics of grape variety, bouquet, body and finish.

*The veins on the leaves are all in puce and of a similar length, which suggests corner-cutting.* ———

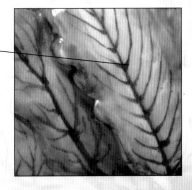

*The leading front paw of this rabbit has a mould-line running along the edge. To leave such a join untrimmed is uncharacteristically clumsy for Chelsea.*

*Paris (Samson) tureen, 19th/20th century, 26 cm (10 in) long, £1,000–£2,000*

# A Bow Quail Pattern Dish

Porcelain decorated with coloured enamels was first produced in England in the late 1740s and 1750s. The earliest European porcelain factories (with the exception of Medici, which was too early) all copied the style we now call Kakiemon. Bow was a rival to Chelsea (*see pages 44–5*), but in fact they served different clientele. Chelsea made for the aristocracy, Bow for the then expanding mid-18th-century middle classes.

Like Chelsea, Bow was making a soft-paste porcelain, although the two are very different. Bow's was a bone-ash formula and contained up to 50 per cent burned ox bones. The potting was on the heavy side and, if one can get any light to shine through it at all, it shows a very deep amber/straw colour. They used several marks, including an anchor and dagger; the Chelsea mark was an anchor alone. This was very small and placed very close to the foot rim, not in the centre of the dish. Most Bow was unmarked.

The early English factories – Chelsea and Bow were both founded around 1745 – became very collectable in the last quarter of the 19th century and a shortage of the original provided a ripe market for the forger. The best known of these is Samson (*see pages 35 and 45*), but there were many others working in Paris and the Herend factory in Hungary was responsible for many more, often very good, reproductions. And this is a very important point to make: most of these copies were not intended to deceive anyone, they were simply copies. The problem of identification developed over time as the original intention was forgotten. The main difference is, of course, the paste or body. Continental copies are in hard paste, not soft.

Bow did a number of designs based on Japanese Kakiemon originals. One of their most famous designs was known as the Quail Pattern: dishes are crisply moulded on the exterior as shells and sit on three seaweed- and shell-encrusted feet. The glaze is quite thick and greenish, and is suffused with numerous minuscule black dots. On unglazed portions, such as the feet, the porcelain body has turned a brown colour, caused by phosphoric acid from the bones reacting with the atmosphere.

The example opposite is not set on shells, but has a flat, unglazed base, which is atypical of Bow. The painter has, at first sight, achieved a reasonable facsimile of the original, but it fails on many counts. As one has to repeat so often, the most important point is the tendency of the copyist to overdo it.

## Japanese Kakiemon wares

The most prized of all porcelains in Europe in the 17th century were the enamelled wares exported from Japan. In fact, Japanese porcelain was the first to come from the East in colours and made an immediate impact when it arrived. At one time it was thought that Kakiemon was the product of one man, then of a family; we now know there was a whole series of kilns working at Arita.

The Japanese started tentatively producing Kakiemon wares in the mid-17th century and by the 1680s were producing superbly balanced designs in jewel-like enamels leaving – always a joy to see – a lot of the white porcelain showing. The usual Kakiemon palette is red, blue, green, yellow and turquoise. Subjects included figures, tigers, *shi-shi* (Buddhist lions), insects, flowers and birds, particularly quail or partridge. This last design was a cult collectable in the 18th century and was imitated at numerous factories including Meissen, Chelsea and Bow.

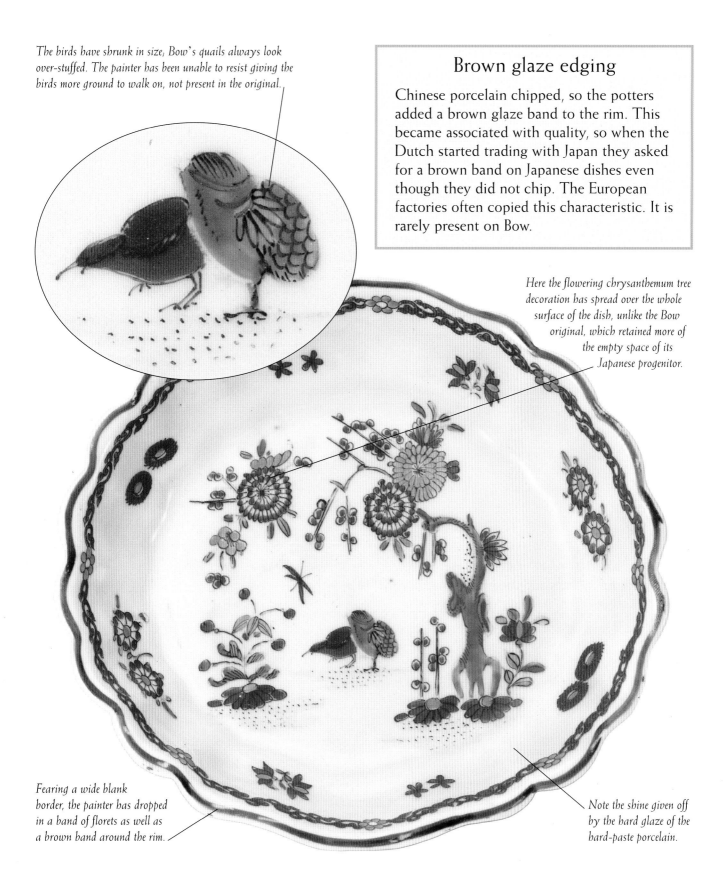

The birds have shrunk in size; Bow's quails always look over-stuffed. The painter has been unable to resist giving the birds more ground to walk on, not present in the original.

## Brown glaze edging

Chinese porcelain chipped, so the potters added a brown glaze band to the rim. This became associated with quality, so when the Dutch started trading with Japan they asked for a brown band on Japanese dishes even though they did not chip. The European factories often copied this characteristic. It is rarely present on Bow.

Here the flowering chrysanthemum tree decoration has spread over the whole surface of the dish, unlike the Bow original, which retained more of the empty space of its Japanese progenitor.

Fearing a wide blank border, the painter has dropped in a band of florets as well as a brown band around the rim.

Note the shine given off by the hard glaze of the hard-paste porcelain.

A Continental copy of a Bow dish, 16.5 cm (6½ in) wide, £80–£120

# BERNARD LEACH POTTERY

## Oriental influences

While many of Leach's works continue the traditions of native English slipware (*see pages 42–3*), the overall impression of his total – and often mediocre – output is Oriental: Japan-style lustrous black *temmoku* glazes, Ming-style celadons, scenes of Buddhist monks silhouetted before mountain peaks, a squiggle or dash of Oriental-looking calligraphy, Song-style bowls and bulbous Korean-style bottles. Leach unquestionably re-invigorated the native Arts and Crafts ethic, but many view his Eastern inclinations themselves as coming close to the 'faking' of a foreign tradition on native English soil.

In 1909 Bernard Leach (1887–1979) sailed to Japan as a student and teacher of graphic art. Eleven years later he returned to England – as a potter. Not any old potter, but as heir-elect to Japan's ancient title of 'Kenzan', an unbroken line of master potters stretching back to the 17th-century potter Ogata Kenzan (1663–1743).

Along with his friend and fellow potter Hamada Shoji (1894–1978) Leach set up a pottery in Cornwall and in the years that followed St Ives became the seedbed of the British Studio Pottery Movement, with Leach, the Potter-Preacher, its beacon light. When not actually making vessels Leach himself was busy lecturing and writing on the state of modern ceramic design and manufacture and on the gulf between current industrial design and Far Eastern aesthetic values. Some of the subsequently famous names associated with the Leach/St Ives group included Michael Cardew, Katherine Pleydell Bouverie and Norah Braden, as well as several members of Bernard Leach's own family.

Some years later, while detained at Her Majesty's pleasure at Fetherstone Prison, Wolverhampton, two men, William Boardman and Vincent Mason, decided to latch on to the St Ives 'tradition'. In a clear 'tribute' to the master they created celadon, brown and black-glazed stoneware pots, marked with imitation St Ives seals and the initials 'BL'. Fresh from the prison kiln, Boardman and Mason's hot 'St Ives' pieces were passed on to the open market where, in 1980 (a year after Leach's death), they surfaced at all four leading London auction houses: Sotheby's Belgravia, Christie's, Phillips and Bonham's. Three months later, after buying a 'Boardman-not-Leach' piece himself, ceramics specialist Richard Dennis became suspicious on seeing a similar bowl coming up at

*This celadon bowl is boldly faceted using a wire or plane, each slice cut strongly, without hesitation and with a disregard for absolute linear accuracy. The result is lively and spontaneous.*

*Cut-sided stoneware bowl by Bernard Leach, 1920, £2,000–£4,000*

# Fetherstone Prison fake

*This colour is often seen on genuine Leach pieces.*

*The shape is Leach-ish, but there is a lack of spontaneity in execution.*

*The unglazed underside has fired to a characteristic orangey red (caused by oxidization or rusting of iron in the body during the firing, an effect much admired in Ming dynasty China and exploited by potters everywhere).*

*The sides are too steep for the 'spring' of the foot so that the bowl just 'sits' rather than reaching out.*

*The impressed mark, immodestly placed well above the foot rim, is far too prominent.*

Phillips. The police were informed and the fakes were exposed. The potters, still 'inside', and their outside go-between, were all charged. Defending them against the charge of faking St Ives pottery, Mason's and Boardman's lawyers argued that there had been no serious intent to deceive, since (quoting their pottery tutor) their ceramic skills were considered to be 'quite hopeless'. The jury thought otherwise. Before sentencing, Judge Solomon wryly remarked that the tutor had clearly underestimated the artistic talents of her captive students. Indeed, Vincent Mason's 'Leach' work actually contributed to his gaining an 'O' Level qualification in ceramics.

In the early 1980s, with genuine Leach bowls typically fetching sums in the mid- to high hundreds, they were certainly worth faking – especially if the Home Office was paying for tuition. (Her Majesty's raw materials were actually paid for by the potters themselves.) Today, some 20 years on, Leach's works often fetch well into the thousands. It is not yet clear whether all the

Fetherstone Prison fakes have been found but, bearing in mind that Leach's huge output includes many second-rate pieces, it's a brave person who dismisses the copy from a photograph alone. However, when giving evidence at the Mason and Boardman case, Bernard Leach's widow (herself a potter) testified that the faked pieces could never have passed for genuine in the eyes of a true ceramics expert.

## Stoneware glazes

Cut-sided forms are characteristic of a large output from the St Ives kilns, reflecting Japanese bowl and bottle shapes. These in turn mirror the wares of the Song dynasty in China (960–1279) when foremost amongst stoneware glazes were a lustrous black and brown (now referred to by the Japanese name *temmoku*) and a whole range of greens (in Europe called celadon).

*Imitation 'Leach' bowl, Fetherstone Prison, c.1980, £50–£100 curiosity value*

# CARLTON WARE

How grand to be a Toucan Just think what Toucan do

*The colour and detail on original toucans is far superior to that of most of the fakes on the market.*

*With its loopy design, the backstamp resembles the Clarice Cliff mark. Fake pieces sometimes have transfers stuck on them, such as the examples below.*

Carlton Ware was first produced in 1890, when James Frederick Wiltshaw went into partnership with two brothers, William Herbert and James Alcock Robinson, and took over the premises of the Carlton Works' factory in Stoke-on-Trent. The partnership did not last for long, however, and after a bitter split, James Wiltshaw became the sole owner of the factory, which remained in family hands for the next 75 years.

The company came into its own during the early 1930s when, inspired by the Jazz Age and the recent discovery of Tutankhamun's tomb, and aware of the success that Wilkinsons were having with Clarice Cliff's brightly-coloured designs, the factory introduced Art Deco and Egyptian ranges with abstract patterns and high-lustre finishes.

From the 1950s Carlton produced a number of humorous advertising figures based on the brilliant, tongue-in-cheek Guinness advertising campaign 'Guinness is Good for You'. Most famous was the toucan depicted in various poses including a flight of three wall plaques in the manner of the more customary ducks. Whereas the advertising pieces have reached cult status, and many of the other lines have become very collectable (a fact that is always of interest to the forger), sadly for Carlton Ware recession in the 1980s put the company out of business.

In 1989 a Staffordshire lorry driver was asked to dispose of the former stock and moulds of the Carlton Ware factory. Instead of disposal he

Carlton Ware
Handpainted
MADE IN ENGLAND
"TRADE MARK"

MADE IN
"TRADE MARK"

Carlton Ware
Handpainted
MADE IN ENGLAND
"TRADE MARK"

*Genuine Guinness toucan, 1950s, £500*

*Genuine moulds from the Carlton Ware factory were discovered at the lorry driver's private factory. His work is easy to spot, however, as it is badly painted, the colours are poor, and the slogans and marks are applied transfers rather than hand-painted or stamped texts.*

decided to enter the ceramics business himself. Eight years later his premises were raided and the police uncovered moulds, transfers and finished goods. He was charged with making counterfeit Carlton Ware toucans and other advertising novelties originally made for the promotion of Guinness stout beer.

He was also charged with producing 'Clarice Cliff' items from the Bizarre range, pieces which, if genuine, would have been worth several hundred pounds and for which he managed to get £50 apiece. Found guilty, he was sentenced to 180 hours community service and was ordered to pay £3,000 costs.

*Fake Guinness toucan, 1990s,*
*£20–£40*

## Clarice Cliff

In common with many of her Tunstall classmates, Miss Cliff left school aged 12, bound for the local Staffordshire ceramic industry. In 1927, after working for over 10 years at Wilkinsons of Burslem, she was promoted to designer/painter. There, with the encouragement of the director Colley Shorter (whom she later married) she created a totally new range of bold and colourful patterns dubbed 'Bizarre'. The patterns were so successful that within a couple of years Cliff was concentrating on design while the 'Bizarre Girls' executed the patterns. Thus the 'Clarice Cliff' facsimile signature continued, becoming a general trade mark and was employed on some of the factory's more conservative designs.

Today, the most highly collected pieces are the bright, jazzy, geometric patterns painted on angular, conical, jet-stream shapes we associate with the early 1930s – Staffordshire Art Deco. Prices for such pieces can reach thousands of pounds.

# EARLY LEAD GLASS

The well-loved story of an Englishman, George Ravenscroft, discovering the secret of making an improved glass lead crystal by incorporating lead oxide in the metal is, sadly, no longer believed. Nevertheless, his reputation for experiments into improving the glass of the late 17th and early 18th century and for producing some of the outstanding pieces of the period remains.

Lead glass has definite advantages. It is, as one might expect, heavier than the former soda glass, is brighter and can be made thicker, making it ideal for deep cutting. Early lead drinking glasses were large and sturdy and a complete change from the light and delicate Continental glass that had previously been current in England. Usual were heavy stems in a form derived from furniture and silver and known as a baluster, a widely spreading blob with the pointed end down. As the glass-blowers became familiar with the ductile nature of the metal, they invented new forms of blobs which are called knops and come in an almost infinite variety of forms. Several on one glass were common and the later the glass, generally speaking, the more elaborate the stem. Collectors are much exercised about the different forms of knop and try and complete collections of every variety. Glass, being transparent, depends on the subtleties of form; how each element relates to another and the overall balance. Copyists can rarely reproduce this harmony.

So good was English glass that it was imported by Dutch engravers and stipplers and the finished product re-imported. There were good engravers in England and there were also indifferent and bad engravers. The difficulty for the collector is that a poor copy of earlier engraving may just look like a not-very-good original. We now know that large quantities of perfectly genuine but plain 18th-century drinking glasses were decorated in the late 19th and early 20th centuries with patterns to

*The heavy round funnel bowl is typical of the period.*

*The rim of the glass foot is folded under.*

*Knops in the stems of 17th- and 18th-century glasses came in a variety of shapes and sizes, including the annulated knop (above) and the basal knop (below).*

*Baluster goblet, c.1695, £1,500–£2,000*

make them more expensive. Most commonly encountered are Jacobite and Williamite glasses. These celebrate the causes of James Stuart (the Old Pretender), his son, Bonnie Prince Charlie (the Young Pretender), and William of Orange. Jacobite glasses were often engraved with a rose, which was the symbol associated with the Old Pretender. Buds are supposed to represent his son. A raft of other emblems, such as caterpillars, butterflies, stars, oak leaves and blackbirds – all of which have been found engraved on glasses – has been interpreted as having Jacobite significance. In all probability, such symbols were simply whims of the engraver, and gave no clue to the political leanings of the drinker.

William of Orange, who ruled England from 1689 to 1702, defeated James II at the Battle of the Boyne, just north of Dublin, on 1 July 1690. The battle was highly significant in British and Irish history, and is still celebrated by the Ulster Unionists. It is likely that they commissioned the glass below on the 200th anniversary of the battle in 1890. It is probable that no glasses purporting to date from the time of the battle are genuine.

## A 'Williamite' glass

*The engraving is similar to that of Franz Tietze (1842–1932), a Bohemian glass engraver who worked in Dublin and whose design notebook is now in the V&A, London.*

*This form of stem is not found on glasses dating from the 17th century.*

*A glass celebrating the Williamite cause and engraved with the king's equestrian portrait and the inscription to: THE GLORIOUS MEMORY OF THE BATTLE OF THE BOYNE, 1ST JULY 1690.*

*It is likely that techniques will soon be developed to enable us to determine when a piece of glass was engraved through changes in the structure of the cut over time or through a difference in the actual wheels leaving characteristic marks. At present, the trained eye, which looks at the stiffness or the dexterity of the hand of the wheel-cutter, is the best guide.*

*Glass commemorating the Battle of the Boyne, c.1890, £300–£500*

# HUMPEN

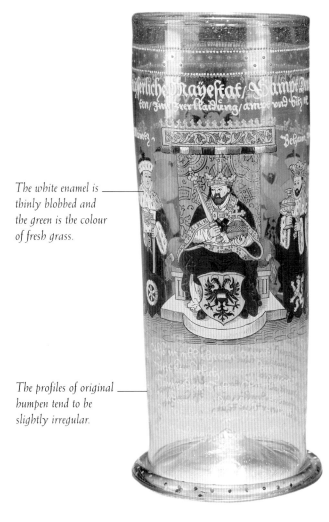

The white enamel is thinly blobbed and the green is the colour of fresh grass.

The profiles of original humpen tend to be slightly irregular.

*The figures are rendered as flat areas of colour, which gives them a certain solidity. There is vigour to the handling of the enamels, note particularly the spontaneity of the writing.*

It is not certain where or when glass was first developed, but western Asia about 5,000 years ago is likely. Its first use was not for vessels but as a substitute for precious stones. Popular belief has it that Arabs lit a fire in the sands and supported their cooking pot on a fluxing material such as soda. The heat melted the flux and sand and produced the first glass. True or not, the discovery would surely have been accidental.

Glass has great advantages for the decorative arts. It can be cast, coloured or clear, engraved with a diamond, cut on a wheel or overlaid with different colours. In addition it can be enamelled.

Enamel is effectively ground glass with a colouring oxide. It was known in Roman times, but fell into disuse until the late 13th century when it reappeared in Italy and spread upward through Europe. Certainly it had reached Germany by 1571, the earliest dated example.

Most of the early surviving enamelled glasses were large drinking vessels with coats of arms, hunting scenes or illustrations from biblical texts. The most common shape is the 'Humpen', a tall, cylindrical beaker for wine or beer, which may be up to 60 cm (2 feet) high. Some have covers.

The colour and consistency of the glass varied because the glass-maker produced a new batch of 'metal', the correct name for the material, daily, varying the precise ingredients going into each 'pot' (the melting furnace).

*Genuine Bohemian enamelled Kurfürstenhumpen, c.1600, 26.3 cm (10¼ in) tall, £7,000–£9,000*

# Imitation humpen

Humpen were made of *Waldglas* (forest glass), so called because it came from the forests of Germany where potash, which was used as the flux, was readily available in its unburnt form of beech or other woods. The glass has a distinctive greenish, yellowish or brownish tinge. The enamel work was done by a separate group of decorators, who painted scenes to order. Most common was the coat of arms of the Holy Roman Emperor. The example shown (*see left*) is known as a *Kurfürstenhumpen*, which literally means 'electors' beaker' and depicts the seven electors of the empire. Other subjects include knights and kings on horseback, falconers and, extremely popular, hunting. This final group is known as *Jagdhumpen*.

The 19th century saw a rise in the appreciation of old glass. Humpen were copied in quite large numbers and can be difficult to tell from the real thing. We can no longer be sure of the intention behind these reproductions; some were simply a celebration of an earlier style, but others were meant to deceive.

*The figures here look as if they have been cut from cardboard. The hunter is standing as if the boar had run up against his sword, rather than the hunter had made a thrust.*

*The metal is of a pinkish tone and has thousands of air bubbles in a spiral twist through the body.*

*The writing has a certain rigidity about it.*

*While the originals are densely decorated, this is too much so.*

*The whole palette is much more subdued than on the original. It lacks the bright egg-yolk yellow, and the green is a dull sage colour.*

## Dating a face

Faces often give away the true date of a piece. The features of this hunter are far too benevolent to belong to a 17th-century character. Indeed it is much more in keeping with the charitable attitudes that are characteristic of the 19th century.

*Imitation German humpen, dated 1624 but actual date is c.1870, 28 cm (11 in) tall, £400–£600*

# Furniture

❈

As the prospective purchaser of a piece of furniture, there is a moment when you either 'put up' (dig deep into your pocket) or 'shut up' (look elsewhere). A huge comfort in this decision process is the security of knowing that what you are about to buy is a good example, that it is 'right' and that you are aware of any alterations or enhancements.

When examining furniture, it is essential that you approach every piece with a good deal of suspicion. Never believe in a piece until you have giving it a very close inspection. Look at it as a whole, and then examine a number of specific attributes.

Firstly, look at the colour. Does it have that wonderful build-up of wax and filth in inaccessible crevices, or is it suspiciously clean? Are there signs of fading, where the piece has been left too long near a window? Is it French polished? Unless it is Edwardian or Continental, then this is unlikely to be the original surface.

Secondly, examine its proportions. Are the legs too heavy in relation to the top? Does it look as if the top and bottom were always together? Do the drawers graduate harmoniously? Is it unusually tall for a piece of its type? Are the bracket feet and handles correct for the period? If in doubt, ask a dealer or the auction house.

After 100 or 200 years of domestic life, you would expect a piece to show certain signs of wear. Look on the bottom of the feet, the underside of drawers, loper rails, locks and catches, and the leading edges of tops. If they are too fresh, watch out! Always take drawers out, open cupboards and, if possible, turn the piece upside down to see whether there are any illogical nail or screw holes, or odd bearers and attachments to the backs.

Finally, assess the quality of the piece. If the carving is crisp, the inlay stunning, the turning incredible, or the use of veneer and selection of timbers breathtaking, then it is more likely that it is 'right'.

# GEORGIAN STOOL

Stools have always been sought after because they are highly portable and cheaper to make than a chair with a back and arms. With all the intervening fluctuations of fashion plus the poor rates of survival, 18th century stools are rare. This coupled with their fashionability makes them a surefire candidate for faking or reproduction.

The example below, which is one of a pair, has a gorgeous green Genoa velvet over-stuffed top and sits on parcel or part-gilt walnut cabriole supports on similarly decorated pad feet. The stool is perfectly proportioned, and designed so that all its various elements are in harmony. The top extends down the sides to cover the seat rails, which are themselves shaped to accommodate unusual helmet-form capitals at the top of each leg. And what good legs! Sturdy yet full of movement; bulbous at the knee and elegant at the ankle.

## Developments in seating

In 17th-century courtly France, the protocol concerning seat furniture was very complex. Only senior courtiers were entitled to use taborets or open stools, while armchairs were reserved for the royal family.
In England, chairs developed from pieces known today as joint or coffin stools. Backs began to be added by the beginning of the 16th century and these, together with the seats, gradually became upholstered (farthingale chairs) and grew arms (wainscot armchairs) as the century progressed.

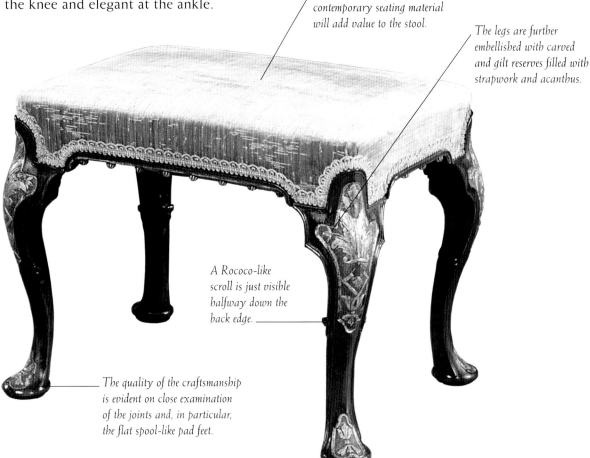

*Having the original or contemporary seating material will add value to the stool.*

*The legs are further embellished with carved and gilt reserves filled with strapwork and acanthus.*

*A Rococo-like scroll is just visible halfway down the back edge.*

*The quality of the craftsmanship is evident on close examination of the joints and, in particular, the flat spool-like pad feet.*

*Georgian stool, 1710, 58 cm (23 in) wide, £6,000–£8,000*

*The timber purports to be walnut, but the colour is too red for this to be likely.*

*This carved cartouche is not only very shallow and weak, but also atypical on a George I walnut chair.*

*The downswept supports are too slender in proportion to the rest of the stool.*

# Georgian or Georgian-style?

The style of this stool appears to be late Queen Anne or early George I. It has a drop-in seat on a concave-sided rectangular frame and shell-carved and husk-hung cabriole supports on shaped flared feet. But examination of the carving, the colour of the wood, and the proportion of the legs to the body should arouse your suspicions. These are confirmed when you turn it upside-down – at best it is a 1920s reproduction.

*Sage dealers used to say a piece 'turned up nice' when they saw only promising signs on turning it upside down, and this is still a good acid test today. If you turn this example, all is revealed: there is no undercutting behind the ears where the cabriole supports join the seat rail; there is no sign of age in the seat rail; and the seat is kept rigid by a modern block.*

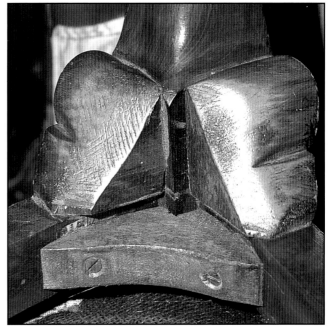

*Imitation Georgian stool, 1920s, £120–£150*

# GAINSBOROUGH ARMCHAIR

A Gainsborough armchair has a rectangular or slightly arched upholstered back, open arms that usually have padded elbow supports, and a padded seat on straight or cabriole supports. They are named after Thomas Gainsborough (1727–88), the consummate portraitist, who frequently painted people sitting on chairs of this type. The chairs were highly sought after in the mid-18th century, and well-made examples, particularly those produced in London, were expensive even then. Purchasers would expect the carving and other workmanship to be of the finest quality.

*All four legs are carved with acanthus, and even the shaped ball feet are embellished with leaves.*

*Contained within each ball foot is an original leather and brass castor.*

## Feet

Look at the amount of wear on the bottom of the front feet. After 250 years of moving furniture across carpets, rugs, floorboards and stone flags you would expect to see distinctive wear along the leading edge of the foot. In this case the wear is regular, suggesting that it has been done with a chisel.

*The carving on the end of the arm support is so crisp and fine that you can practically trace the veins in the leaves.*

*One of a pair of genuine Gainsborough armchairs, c.1750, price for both £40,000*

*Turn the chair upside down and, if you can, peel back the hessian bottom covering to expose as much of the rail as you dare. On this example you can see a brand new machine-made block, which might be a later replacement but allied to the new-looking rails should lead you to the conclusion that the chair is a copy dating from around 1900.*

## Provincial or reproduction?

You should be immediately suspicious of this example. The shape of the chair is not typically 18th-century, and the carving – which includes a long trail of acanthus with rather illogical beads on the downswept arm supports – does not reach the standards expected of a London-made chair. To confirm whether it is an 18th-century chair made in the provinces, or a later reproduction, you also need to turn it upside down and examine the blocks and feet.

*The arms and downswept arm supports are too slender for a period London-made chair.*

*The front legs are not in proportion with the rest of the chair, and the carving on the knees and feet is not of 18th-century quality.*

*The back feet are of a different style to the front feet, indeed the back feet are uncarved.*

*One of a pair of imitation Gainsborough armchairs, c.1900, price for both £2,000–£4,000*

# CARVED GILTWOOD MIRRORS

This mirror was supplied to Charles, Fifth Duke of Bolton (d.1765) for his stately home, Hackwood Park in Hampshire. It is in the late George II 'antique' manner, which was introduced by the architect John Vardy (d.1765).

The carving is of the finest quality – a giltwood and gesso cresting is flanked by pierced Rococo 'C' and 'S' scrolls, above the rectangular plate. The pierced sides are hung with bell flower swagging, and the apron (the bottom of the mirror) has another central cartouche filled with a Venus shell as if in reflection of the shell in the cresting above. The Roman acanthus wreathing and ornament is derived from the Inigo Jones style and the husk-festooned frame can be traced back to the frontispiece of Vardy's 1744 publication *Some Designs of Mr. Inigo Jones and Mr. William Kent*.

Probably finished around 1760, this mirror would have been considered extremely desirable by the dilettantes who had travelled to Rome on the Grand Tour.

*The honeyed tones of the gilding have mellowed over the years in a way that is impossible to reproduce artificially.*

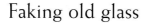

*The quality of the carving stands out on the shell-shaped cresting, which is enclosed by a canopy of scrolls and leaves.*

## Faking old glass

The colour of silvering and the state of an early glass plate itself can be reproduced artificially. 'Spotted' silvering is much sought after by the connoisseur, who will pay more for an original plate in poor condition than a re-silvered plate, or a replaced reproduction plate that has been made to look old.

*Genuine 18th-century giltwood mirror, c. 1760, 185 x 97 cm (73 x 38 in), £95,000*

# Victorian reproduction

Purporting to be from a similar, or slightly later
date to the example opposite, this mirror also has
a rectangular plate and displays apparently
virtuoso Rococo wood carver's skills. But if you
turn the piece over, the modern fittings and lack
of detail and undercutting suggest that it was
probably made in the late 19th century by a
skilled carver.

*The elaborately carved tri-form cresting lacks the sort of
nervous movement – a 'tremble' in each of the asymmetric
pieces of leafage – that you would expect from a genuine
Rococo piece. Instead it looks suspiciously stiff.*

*The honey-gilt surface has a rather fresh
appearance. Sections of the bole used to seal
the gesso are showing through, suggesting that
it has been artificially rubbed in a restorer's
workshop some time in the last 10 years.*

*If you turn the mirror over, the lack of
undercutting or hand-chiselled work behind
each of the delicate outer edges is plain to
see. This is particularly obvious in the
pierced sections of the outset corners.*

*The mirrored plate is
secured by a single
modern mirror pin.*

*The hanging wire is
attached by modern
fixings, with no
evidence of any old
fixings in the vicinity.*

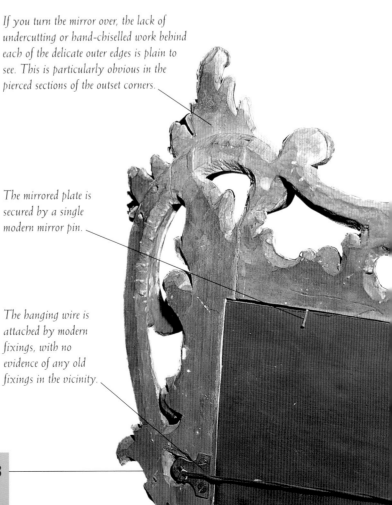

*Imitation 18th-century giltwood mirror, c. 1890,
91 x 61 cm (36 x 24 in), £5,000 a pair*

# CHINESE CHIPPENDALE ARMCHAIR

*The carving in the middle of the back rail is remarkable for its detail.*

*The fretted back is put together in a way that is typical of the period.*

*The wood used in an old repair to the back leg has faded at a different rate to that of the main body of the chair.*

What could better epitomize 18th-century Chinese Chippendale taste, than this delightful pair of armchairs? Each has a rectangular Chinese fret-filled back and sides, an overstuffed seat on elaborate pierced square front supports and turned back supports. Surely, you would say, these must be the genuine article? Well, you would be half right, for if we take the example below, there are certain details that reassure us that this chair is of the correct date and period. The foliate and scroll carving on the tablet in the middle of the back rail is convincing as is the construction of the fretted back itself. If the chair is turned upside down and the rails, blocks and stretchers examined, the underside of the seat rail is constructed in 18th-century style and shows its age. Even better, if you look on the underside of the front leg you will find a quadrant block – another period feature. It is not unusual for a 200-year-old chair to have been damaged at some point in its history, and this example has a repair on its back leg. Again, this might reassure the critical eye of an expert.

If we turn now to the other 'identical' chair (*right*), it begins to be apparent that this is not an old chair, but one that has been made to match

## Quadrant blocks

The construction method of the legs also reveals a lot about the date of a piece of furniture. In this case, two pierced and carved sections form the front and the sides of the leg, which are joined by a quadrant block, the correct method for the period.

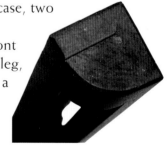

*Pair of Chinese Chippendale armchairs, c. 1765,*
*£10,000–£15,000*

# Reproduction armchair

the original, probably in around 1900. The carving on the tablet at the top of the back rail is convincing, but not quite up to scratch, while the fretted back differs slightly from the original, its supposed twin. If you look on the underside, there is no evidence of old open stretchers, instead a much later brace is revealed. Similarly, the front feet have been made out of a solid piece, with no quadrant blocks, and show few signs of use.

If you owned a grand country house in 1900 and you wanted six or eight of these chairs to go into your saloon and you only had four old ones, it would not have been difficult to go to a London craftsman and say make two or four additional copies, exactly like the old ones. They had the quality of timber and considerable skills and modest workshop charges that would enable very close copies to have been made, which is what has happened in this particular instance. Some 80 or 90 years of being polished, abused and dragged across floors makes it increasingly difficult for us today to correctly distinguish the Edwardian copy from the 18th-century original.

Both of these chairs come from the collection of Lord Leverhulme, and are on view at the Lady Lever Art Gallery in Port Sunlight, Merseyside. Why not pay a visit and see if you can tell the original from the copy? Just don't try turning them upside-down in a public gallery!

*The carving is not as detailed as that on the original. Also, the colour and construction of the fretted back is not exactly the same.*

*The underside features rails that are kept braced by a solid Edwardian-type winged block.*

*The front leg has been made out of a single piece of wood, and shows a good deal less wear.*

*You would expect to find 18th-century rails, blocks and stretchers when you turned the chair upside down, but this example is constructed in a later style.*

*Pair of reproduction Chinese Chippendale armchairs, c.1900, £2,000–£4,000*

# CLASSICAL COMMODE

*The satin-, hare- and purplewood veneers are well-drawn and figured to please the eye.*

*The elaborate marquetry decoration is of a very high quality and is exquisitely arranged.*

*The deal back on the 18th-century example, although with unorthodox framed construction with three tenoned stiles (vertical framing members in a piece of panelling), is at least convincing.*

*This ormolu mount appears to have organically sprouted out of the timber.*

In France the term 'commode' is applied to a chest of drawers that evolved into a grand piece of case furniture that was always fitted with drawers and was sometimes enclosed by cupboards. From the reign of Louis XIV (1643–1715) to that of Louis XVI (1774–92), the commode became increasingly enriched and ornamented.

In Britain, fashionable furniture-makers often mirrored Continental styles and influences. The example illustrated above is a fine commode made in England in around 1775. The frame is made from deal and mahogany, and veneered in pear and other fruitwoods, sycamore, harewood, holly, tulipwood, purplewood, kingwood, East Indian satinwood and box. Further embellishment is in

the form of crisply cast ormolu mounts. Probably commissioned by the first Lord Ashburton, this commode was sold by Lord Henry Thynne in 1899 for £420 and was bought in 1904 by Lord Lever for £750.

The marquetry decoration is largely in sycamore with tulipwood crossbanding and partly stained sycamore stringing. The top is filled with a fan of large gadroons outlined with green stained stringing all in sycamore radiating from a centre of sycamore and pear. The spandrels between the gadroons are filled with bell-flowers of green stained pear on a purplewood ground.

If we compare this with the example on the page opposite, apart from the configuration of the

*Commode, c.1775,*
*86 cm (34 in) high, £30,000–£40,000*

# Reconstructed commode

legs, the demi-lune outline and Neoclassical style are quite similar. Can we assume from this visual similarity that they date from the same period? Watch out, because this piece certainly does not date from the third quarter of the 18th century, at least not in its present form. The doors appear to have been adapted from an older piece of furniture; although newly veneered in front, they retain the original thicker mahogany veneer on the backs. This re-use of older pieces accounts for the different construction of the right-hand door from the left-hand door. Several features of this later commode underscore its late 19th-century origin. There is an overall lack of any sense of scale to the design, much of the marquetry is poorly executed and the back and underside of the remodelled commode reveal it has been constructed in an illogical manner.

It just goes to show that even if the object is grand and stands in regal splendour in someone's drawing room, you need to be even more eagle-eyed in analyzing the good and bad points to make sure that you are not being sold a reconstructed fake.

*Much of the marquetry is pinched and scrawny.*

*The massive bell-flower filled spandrels are completely out of proportion with the rest of the piece.*

*A new veneer has been added to an old pair of doors – they retain the original thicker mahogany veneer on the backs.*

*The apron and legs are coarse and badly executed.*

*The back of the later commode is a muddle of rabbets or rebates (joints between two pieces of timber where a groove is cut into one piece to receive the other) and nails. Even to the untrained eye it looks like a complete mess!*

## The British commode

In Britain, the term commode is often used to describe a small piece of furniture that encloses a chamber pot or washbasin and stands beside a bed. Sometimes you can sit on the commode (some have built in arms) and sometimes you merely have a pull-out chamber pot which is disguised effectively in the piece of furniture.

*Reconstructed commode, late 19th-century,
84 cm (33 in) high, £6,000–£8,000*

# BONHEUR DU JOUR

The name *bonheur du jour*, adopted in mid-18th-century France for small feminine writing tables surmounted by a cabinet, could be translated as 'daytime delight' in so far as the desk might be used for penning a billet-doux. In Chippendale's *Cabinet-Maker's Directory*, third edition (1762), there is reference to a piece of this type as 'A Ladie's writing table and bookcase', and a variety of other names were used in Hepplewhite & Co.'s *The Cabinet Makers and Upholsterers Guide* (1788) and Thomas Sheraton's *The Cabinet Makers & Upholsterer's Drawing Book* (1793). It is interesting to note that in the 18th century the main living room fulfilled a dual function of library and drawing room, so elegant pieces of furniture at which a lady (*bonheur du jour*) or gentleman (*escritoire*) could quite congruously attend to correspondence were much in demand.

This piece is made of satinwood, and has an elaborately shaped gallery with an exaggerated back panel centred by an oval vignette filled with *amorini* (baby cupids) inside a garland – a theme repeated on the two doors below. Its hinged writing surface opens in conjunction with a frieze drawer, which offers support. It was made around 1790 and conforms to the 18th-century ideal epitomized in England by the Sheraton style. It is delicate, beautifully finished and pleasing on the eye, conjuring up the elegant interiors of the Age of Enlightenment.

The 18th-century *amorini* (baby cupids) have been well drawn.

The Georgian lock is of a brass-and-steel 'two tumbler' type.

Note the mellow colour of the satinwood, and the overall harmony of the piece.

## Drawers

The real clues to a piece of furniture's origins often lie within. If you compare the drawer linings of these two pieces, those in the 18th-century example are wafer thin, while the early 20th-century example's are comparatively thick. Also, look at the joints. Early dovetailing was done by hand, while later joints were often machine-made.

*Genuine bonheur du jour, c.1790, £12,000*

# Edwardian reproduction

This piece also echoes the Sheraton style, with a superstructure flanked by cupboards painted in the Classical manner, but it has an overall 'gingery' colour, which suggests that it is made from East Indian satinwood, an inferior material. The colour of the wood is not decisive, however, as some genuine 18th-century pieces have been inexpertly repolished to the 'wrong' colour. Further clues that all is not what it seems can be found in the painted areas, which have been executed in the manner of Angelica Kauffmann, an 18th-century artist whose style was much in vogue towards the end of the 19th century on both furniture and ceramics (*see page 41*).

The Edwardian piece is fitted with inferior machine-made 'catches'.

The wood is a 'gingery' colour, suggesting that it could be made from East Indian satinwood.

*On close inspection the larger panels are covered in artificial 'craquelure', a minute meshwork of cracks developing naturally over time, and reproduced here in paint. Also, the overall brushwork is loose and unconvincing.*

*Imitation bonheur du jour, c.1905, £4,000*

# A GEORGIAN QUARTETTO OF TABLES

The darling of an English drawing room – a delightful quartetto of tables. But is it Georgian or Edwardian reproduction? First impressions are that both of these sets look right and fit well together, but on closer inspection one is revealed to be 100 years older than the other.

Nests of three or four tables that slot into each other when not in use were an ingenious and space-saving invention of the late 18th-century. The sets have remained popular, and today they are very ready sellers at auction. The original Georgian tables, such as those shown in the example below, were usually restrained in appearance. Styles became more elaborate during the 19th century, but there was a return to simplicity during the Edwardian era. This means

*The top table in a set is often the lightest, because it has had more exposure to the sun. In this case, however, there is no sign of bleaching, suggesting that the tables have been kept away from direct sunlight.*

*The cock beading stands proud of the main surface on this example.*

*The turning on the twin column supports is generally of a far higher quality than you would expect to find on an Edwardian example.*

*Georgian stretcher rails are nearly always made of three-ply.*

*Georgian quartetto of tables, c.1805, £6,000–£8,000*

# An Edwardian reproduction

that it is sometimes difficult to distinguish between the two periods. There are, however, some clues to help the prospective buyer.

The set of Georgian mahogany quartetto tables is simple but elegant, with a raised ebony cock bead on ring-tuned twin column supports. Rosewood and mahogany are the most common woods to be used for such tables, and early pieces are more likely to be made from quality materials. The size of the tables is also significant.

The Edwardian set (*right*) conforms closely to the Georgian pattern with four tops of rectangular outline, each with a satinwood cross-banded surface contained by ebony and boxwood lines, the outer edge being neatly contained by a cock bead. Normally on Georgian examples, the cock bead stands quite proud, acting as a mini gallery to stop a glass or dish from being accidentally knocked off. On this Edwardian example the cock beading is, if anything, rather shallow. Also, the timber is inferior and the quality of the cross-banding is not particularly high.

Next turn your attention to the turning on the legs. Here we have three neatly turned rings, but on the Georgian example the turning is much more vigorous and better drawn.

An incredibly useful tip to determine the 18th-century from the 19th-century copy in this type of table is the three-ply test. Turn the Edwardian table upside-down and look at the narrow stretcher rail between the supports. This serves a dual function of stiffening up the table frame and restraining the three smaller tables from shooting out the other side when they are slid into position. On the Edwardian example this piece of timber is quite obviously solid, while on the Georgian set it is made of three-ply. Do not always take this as gospel because, of course, the original three-ply rail might have got damaged and replaced with a solid piece, but it is a very useful indication.

*The stretcher rails are made from one piece of wood.*

*The turning on the supports is not as animated.*

*The gingery colour of the wood indicates it is of poor quality.*

## Cock beading

A moulding that is normally applied to the edges of drawers, cock beading was inset into quartetto table tops to stop objects from being knocked off. It was often more prominent on Georgian tables than Edwardian ones.

*Edwardian quartetto of tables, c.1905,*
*£1,000–£1,500*

# PAINTINGS, DRAWINGS AND SCULPTURE

❖──◆──❖

Fakes have infiltrated every corner of the art market, but it is the forgers of paintings who consistently catch the public's imagination, and who are thought of as lovable rogues who have fooled the experts, rather than criminals intent on making a fast buck from an unsuspecting buyer. The problem is not a new one – it emerged as soon as art was considered to have a value. During the Roman Empire, for example, Greek statuary was in great demand, and difficulties in supplying the genuine article led to workshops springing up in Rome that produced Greek-style pieces.

Since the 16th-century, artists have studied under a master and learnt to copy works before becoming studio assistants. Geniuses such as Michelangelo and Brueghel reproduced the works of their predecessors, a fact that still leads to some confusion.

The birth of the modern art market can be dated back to the 18th century, when young aristocrats started to collect works of art on the Grand Tour. Many of the souvenirs they brought home turned out to be fakes. The market quickly expanded, and soon it was being flooded with copies of the works of 17th-century masters such as Frans Hals and El Greco.

The 20th century saw an enormous increase in the value of paintings, and an equal increase in the number of fakes produced. Van Meegeren confessed to forging Vermeers in order to evade charges of collaboration with the Nazis; Elmyr de Hory forged the works of Van Dongen and then persuaded the artist to sign them; Tom Keating became a television star after confessing to forging thousands of artworks; and Drewe and Myatt were imprisoned for forging the works of artists such as Graham Sutherland and Ben Nicholson and then placing false authenticating documents in the national archives.

# BENNER STILL-LIFE

*The quality of this painting, which is signed by the artist, becomes obvious when it is compared with the fake opposite.*

Some of the most successful fakes are produced in Italy, where there is a tradition of the skills necessary to trick the unwary. The picture on the right is not a copy, but a real painting made 20 or 30 years ago in the manner of the 19th-century French flower painter Jean Benner. The real Benner, shown above, is a brilliant riot of flowers – and frankly the fake one is rather good too!

To tell the two paintings apart, look at the back. With the painting on the right, the tape that seals the stretcher to the back of the frame has been 'tea stained' to make it look old. Even the nails (these kinds of 'brads' were not made until the 20th century) have been dipped in acid to make them seem rusty. The stretcher itself has been randomly bashed with a hammer and stained to give an impression of age. The final give-away is the staining on the back of the canvas, which has been done to make it look as though age and damp have left tidal marks – convincing at first sight until one runs one's hand over it. Feel the soft 'nap' of a brand new cheap canvas and the fake is betrayed – the real thing should feel rough and bald.

Returning to the front of the picture, check the surface. There are cracks in the paint surface, and at the very edges of the stretcher one can see the finer 'craquelure' in the underpaint to the sides. As one layer dries upon another, the different rates at which the paint dries make little tectonic platelets split away from one another forming delicate cobwebs. Over 150 years this happens naturally in many paintings, but in this case the ageing process has been accelerated by baking the painting in an Italian pizza oven! More recently, advances in the manufacture of cracking acrylic paint have enabled fakers to do without the oven.

As always, the real test is to look at the picture as a work of art. Most convincing fakes might pass on their own, but put them next to the real thing and the sheer quality of the original will shine through. An experienced expert should be able to tell a fake without having an original on hand with which to compare it, but many people might be fooled by these clever forgeries that used to sell in London salerooms for large sums of money only 20 years ago.

One final tip is to give the picture a good sniff. Age has its own musty bouquet, which is impossible to reproduce, but a recent fake will smell of chemicals and varnish.

*Still-life by Jean Benner, 1866, £150,000*

The crackled effect on the painting's surface has been artificially produced by baking it.

The back of the canvas feels rough because it has not been worn down with age.

The nails cannot be original as this type was not produced until the 20th century.

The stretcher and canvas have been stained to make them look older than they really are.

## Jean Benner

Jean Benner (1836–1906) was a traditionalist when compared to contemporaries such as Monet or Manet; indeed his works were exhibited at the Paris Salon, the institution that proved so elusive to the Impressionists. Well-known during his lifetime, by the mid-20th century he had fallen into obscurity. Today, a copy of one of his works would attract little attention on the art market, but could be expected to make a reasonable profit for the forger.

*Still-life in the style of Jean Benner, mid-20th century, £300*

# VAN GOGH'S SUNFLOWERS

*There are a total of nine sunflower paintings by van Gogh, three of which display 14 flowers. The authenticity of this example, which hangs in the National Gallery, London, is not in question.*

*The artist has clearly signed the painting on the side of the vase.*

The longer a fake has remained hidden, the more difficult it is to expose. In the complex case of one of the most famous paintings in the world, van Gogh's *Sunflowers*, sold at auction in 1987 for a record £24.75 million, the truth may never be known. The picture was sold at the height of the demand for French Impressionist paintings, and was bought by Yasuda, a huge Japanese insurance company. Since then, experts from France, Italy and Britain have asserted that the Yasuda picture is a copy painted by Claude Emile Schuffenecker, a French artist whom they suspected of being a forger, at the turn of the century.

The problem stems from the fact that records show van Gogh painted only two large paintings of sunflowers and then copied them, making four in all. The Yasuda picture is a fifth, so where does it come from? Defending the picture is Bogomila Welsh-Ovcharov, a Canadian expert in van Gogh. She asserts that Schuffenecker, a dealer as well as an artist, bought the painting in 1894 from van Gogh's sister-in-law, Jo Bonger, through the widow of Père Tanguy, so it must be genuine.

The problems in deciding between the two are endless, and the debate continues. The fact that there are multiple versions of the picture mean

*Sunflowers by Vincent van Gogh, c. 1888, in excess of 30 million*

*Some experts have suggested that this painting, now owned by the Yasuda insurance company, is a poor copy of the painting opposite, executed by Claude Emile Schuffenecker.*

*This stem appears to grow through the leaf, a botanical impossibility not seen in the original.*

*The composition is identical to the National Gallery version, but is unsigned.*

*The outline of the vase is very stiff. On the left-hand example the artist has clearly modified its line to avoid this flatness.*

that it is not always clear which pictures are which in the records and correspondence; to confuse matters more, the Yasuda picture, if it is a fake, was done shortly after the originals were painted, so the forensic dating of the materials might not prove conclusive. What is certain, is that in 1901 the painting was loaned to the Bernheim-Jeune gallery in Paris by Schuffenecker, and that 11 other alleged van Gogh fakes appeared at the same exhibition. The matter may never be resolved. Look at the two illustrations and ask yourself this – is the Yasuda picture good enough to have been painted by Van Gogh?

## Vincent van Gogh

During a working life of roughly 10 years, Vincent van Gogh produced more than 800 paintings and 700 drawings. The sheer size of his output, along with a general lack of documentation, has aroused the suspicions of the experts. Today there are obvious gains to be had from successfully faking a van Gogh, but one has to wonder why in the 1890s a forger would bother with an artist who only sold one painting during his life.

*Sunflowers by Vincent van Gogh, 1889, £24.75 million*

# STUDY FOR THE MASQUE OF CUPID

The great Victorian artist Sir Edward Coley Burne-Jones, Bt., ARA (1833–98) had a good friend and neighbour, a brilliant photographer called Frederick Hollyer (1837–1933). Hollyer was allowed to take his choice of drawings from Burne-Jones' studio and to photograph them to produce, with Burne-Jones' approval, incredibly convincing facsimiles he called 'platinotypes'. The process was invented by William Willis in 1837, using light shone though a negative to produce, after developing, platinum deposited onto the paper, almost indistinguishable from pencil.

The drawing below by Burne-Jones is of his mistress, Maria Zambaco, a very passionate and beautiful expatriate Greek. Victorian London society was scandalized by their relationship, as was his intimate circle of artist friends and patrons, who gossiped freely. In response Burne-Jones made this drawing of Maria, intimidated on both sides by coarse faces signifiying crudity (Crudelitas) and spitefulness (Saevitia).

As the original drawing is in the collection of Plymouth Museum and Art Gallery in England, alarm bells started ringing when the work opposite appeared in a recent sale in New York, described by the experts as by Burne-Jones. There is no doubt about the original, which was exhibited during the artist's lifetime.

*The graphite on the paper will shine if it is placed under a strong light held at an angle.*

*The back of the original is inscribed 'Hollyer sells reproductions of this and had the copyright'.*

*This inscription does not appear on the facsimile, and so must have been added later.*

Study for the Masque of Cupid *by Burne-Jones, 1870, £100,000*

*The left side of this platinotype has been over exposed, a fact that the faker has attempted to disguise by going over the area with a pencil.*

*The inscription had not been added to the drawing when this photograph was taken.*

Hollyer often made his facsimiles the same size as the originals. They were never meant to replace the drawings, but were simply tools to introduce the artist to a wider audience. The photographs sold well and were obviously treasured by their owners as many of them have survived to this day.

Because they were made contemporaneously with the originals, Hollyer's works have a convincing 'age' to them. They can sometimes be spotted by unframing them and holding them up to the light at an oblique angle. The platinotype has no 'sheen', typical of the graphite on the surface of an original. There are some that have been gone over with pencil by skilled and unscrupulous hands, however, and these create real problems, especially as there is no *catalogue raisonné* of Burne-Jones' drawings that gives their whereabouts. These pictures, once copies, are now fakes.

Often the platinotype has Hollyer's studio stamp on the back, but this may have been removed or covered over. The only sure test is very carefully to examine the drawing, for Burne-Jones was rarely, if ever, crude.

## Frederick Hollyer

Hollyer was the youngest son of a line engraver and fine art publisher. He took up photography in around 1860 and established a business reproducing works of art. For relaxation he photographed people at his London studio at 9 Pembroke Square, Kensington, and his portraits were also much admired.

He is best known for his photographs of the Pre-Raphaelite group of artists and their works. His obituary in *The Times* stated, 'He is said to have done as much for their [the Brotherhood's] popularity by reproducing their work as Ruskin did with the pen....With Burne-Jones...his collaboration – for it amounted to that – was particularly close. He photographed their work at different stages – the prints often suggesting modifications to the artists – and his collection of negatives must contain some interesting records of early states.'

*Crudelitas and Saevitia a platinotype by Hollyer after Burne-Jones, 1870–1900, £1,000*

# FRITH'S THE RAILWAY STATION

*Frith's portrayal of Paddington Station was
hailed by John Ruskin as the art of the future.*

*Frith's works were
thickly painted, unlike
the Sotheby's picture.*

*Frith made himself one of the
wealthiest artists of his day by
selling the copyright to his works
along with the paintings.*

In Sotheby's Belgravia in 1980 the late art dealer
Jeremy Maas was viewing a sale. There he saw a
painting catalogued as the work of William Powell
Frith (1819–1909) called *The Railway Station*. The
estimate was £80,000–£120,000, but Sotheby's
hoped it might reach £200,000. Only one other
Victorian picture had ever made so much, but *The
Railway Station* was such a famous and important
work that Sotheby's had high hopes for it. It was
the star of the sale.

Maas believed it to be a fake of the original
painting, which is now in the Royal Holloway and
Bedford College near London. The fake was
certainly signed and dated 1862 by Frith, but the
paint surface was very flat, with none of the
thicker paint of which Frith was fond.

As luck would have it, Sotheby's had hung a
painting next to it that gave Maas a clue as to who

*The Railway Station by William Powell Frith,
1862, in excess of £1 million*

the real artist was. This was *A Painter's First Work* by Marcus Stone (1840–1921), and by a further extraordinary coincidence it was painted in the same year, 1862. Maas was thus able to compare the two pictures minutely and exactly, judging the handling of the paint to be very similar.

Marcus Stone grew up next door to the English author Charles Dickens. When his father died, Dickens found employment for Stone as the illustrator of his *Great Expectations* and *Our Mutual Friend*. However, the drawings were not a success.

It is one thing to know the truth, but now Maas had to prove it. He had read deeply around the subject of Victorian pictures, and found a mention of the Sotheby's picture in *The Journals of Walter White*, who in 1862 was secretary to the Royal Society. White had visited Stone in May 1862 and 'found him copying Frith's picture of a railway station'. The figures in the picture 'were outlined by an engraver's outliner who can do nothing else'.

Maas now had his proof, but before he could draw Sotheby's attention to it he had to consider who might have signed the copy and made it a fake. Given the attitudes of the day, when artists employed many assistants in their studios, he thought it was possible 'that Frith would consider that merely adding a signature and dating it sufficient evidence that he had "finished" the picture'. Thus we have an example of an artist who connived at the faking of his own painting!

Maas notified the saleroom in good time of his doubts, but the picture was not withdrawn from sale. A statement was issued by the saleroom to the effect that the picture was 'if not entirely from the hand of Frith, at the very least finished and polished by the artist'. However, even if this had been true it was too late, for by now a journalist had contacted Maas and on the morning of the sale the news broke. The picture did not sell.

## Artists who have connived with their fakers

Most artists would be outraged if somebody attempted to forge their work, but occasionally they have connived with their fakers either, like Frith, by signing or otherwise authenticating a work that wasn't by their hand or by signing blank pieces of paper that they know will be filled later. One of the biggest scandals of the 20th century concerned the lithographs of the artist and flamboyant self-promoter Salvador Dalí (1904–89). It has been estimated that some 100,000 lithographs bearing the signature of the Spanish Surrealist have been sold throughout the world since the 1980s, many of which had never been near the artist. The scandal did not cease after Dalí's death; 10,000 illicit prints were seized in Hawaii in the 1990s, but a court there declared that they could be sold to the public as copies instead of ordering their destruction.

The opposite has also been known to occur – artists have been known to repudiate their own works, probably because they did not like the end result or because they were disappointed about the prices raised at auction. One such example is the Italian metaphysical artist Giorgio de Chirico, who declared some of his sculptures as forgeries and had them seized. When the case came to court in 1969 it was revealed that de Chirico had signed a legal contract ordering the sculptures to be produced. Likewise, Maurice de Vlaminck was fined for refusing to authenticate some genuine works that he no longer liked.

# 'MARBLE' RELIEF OF NELSON

*While marble has natural streaks of colour, these striations have obviously been man-made.*

*The surface of the composite is granular, unlike marble.*

*The inscription is intended to appeal to those interested in marine memorabilia.*

ENGLAND EXPECTS EVERY MAN WILL DO HIS DUTY

Somewhere in Britain, now, is a small workshop producing scores of fake marble and bronze relief sculptures. Stored carefully within, the perpetrators have amassed a collection of moulds of reliefs by some of the great sculptors of the Victorian era. Nearby is a stack of new frames, and besides the casting apparatus and materials there are paper tape, nails, various stains and chemicals – the antiquing paraphernalia of the faker. The reliefs are distributed at car-boot fairs and provincial auctions, often selling for hundreds of pounds. Some are passably convincing.

The casting material in the fake illustrated here is a composite of marble powders and resin. The work is after John Edward Carew (1785–1868),

OCTOBER 1805

We must never forget those who gave their lives at Trafalgar, when our boats were made of wood and our men were made of iron.

For God, King and Country
Rear Admiral James Dawton

*As it is set in the base of Nelson's column, the original bronze relief has no plaque on its back. Here, however, the unsuspecting buyer is presented with yet more moving prose.*

*Composite relief depicting the death of Nelson, late 20th century, £30–£40*

and depicts the death of Nelson at the Battle of Trafalgar. The original is the great bronze relief that decorates the base of Nelson's column in Trafalgar Square, London, and dates from 1850. The image shows England's hero mortally wounded on the deck of the *Victory*. By the time that Nelson died, at 4.30pm on 21 October 1805, he knew that the epic battle against the French and Spanish fleets had been won. Beneath the relief is the famous message, which he had signalled to the fleet that morning: 'England expects every man will do his duty.'

The first thing to look at to spot the fake is the marble itself. The composite has a very grainy surface, not smooth. The grey stripes, put in the composite to resemble natural colour differences in marble, look contrived. The whole thing looks just a little too clean and perfect.

The back of the plaque itself commonly has a small fake medallion with the impression of an authentic looking device set into the back. In this case there is a fake inscription on the back with a quotation:

October 1805
We must never forget those who
gave their lives at Trafalgar when
our boats were made of wood and
our men were made of iron.

These reliefs will continue to be made until their makers receive a visit from the police and have their operations closed down – beware!

## Frames

The frames of these marble reliefs are usually the biggest give-away. They are painted over with a stained varnish to give an impression of age, needed because they are made new in the Far East in great quantities. Turn the frame over and you will notice the tape sealing the back is stained with tea, and rubbed to distress it. The nails securing the relief in the frame are often new, but made rusty and old-looking with acid.

# HAN VAN MEEGEREN

The Last Supper, *which was painted in 1941 during the Nazi occupation of Holland, was sold to van Beuningen, a famous Dutch collector. In retrospect it is easy to see that the painting lacks Vermeer's luminosity of colour, his subtle graduations in tone, and his masterful grasp of texture, composition and space.*

The story of Han van Meegeren is one of the most extraordinary in the history of fakes. He was born in Deventer, east of Amsterdam, Holland, in 1889, the third child of Roman Catholic parents. In 1907 he went to Delft University to study architecture, but after six years he decided to concentrate on drawing and painting. For the next 19 years he was part of the Dutch art world – exhibitions were held of his paintings, he joined art societies and contributed to the conservative art magazine *De Kemphaan*. He also divorced his first wife and married the actress Jo Oerlemans during this period. But in the autumn of 1932, irritated by the lack of attention that he was receiving from art critics, he decided to leave Holland for the south of France.

Once there, he began to plot his revenge. Having failed to sell four paintings in the style of Frans Hals (*see page* 87), he decided to fake a Vermeer. He took four years to research his subject, during which time he had many obstacles to overcome. First, he had to learn to paint in the style of the great Delft master, then he had to study the tools used in the 17th century – he learnt to mix his own paints and to use badger-hair brushes. Realizing that he would need to work on an old canvas, he bought *The Raising of Lazurus* by a contemporary of Vermeer, Hendrik

The Last Supper *by van Meegeren in the style of Vermeer, 1940–41, £30,000–£40,000*

## Jan Vermeer

Very little is known about Vermeer, which is one of the reasons why van Meegeren was so successful in forging his works. He was born in Delft in 1632, was married with 11 children, and lived with his mother-in-law, Maria Thins. He must have had financial difficulties during his life as he paid his baker with paintings. A slow worker (fewer than 40 paintings are generally accepted as his), his genius was not recognized during his lifetime, and when he died in 1675 his family was plunged into poverty.

Girl with a Pearl Earring, *one of Vermeer's most famous paintings, is a touching portrait of an unknown model. The serenity of the work and the way that it fills the viewer's mind with questions are typical of the master, but were never successfully recreated by van Meegeren.*

Hondius, and stripped it. In 1936 he started work on *Christ at Emmaus*, perhaps his most successful painting, which he finished the following year.

In order to artificially age the painting, and to make sure that it passed the alcohol test, he dipped his brush alternately in paint and a mixture of phenolformaldehyde and lilac oil. He then baked the painting in an oven.

Once finished, van Meegeren employed a lawyer to approach Dr Bredius with the painting, and to tell the respected art historian and expert on Vermeer that he was representing an old Italian family who needed to raise some money. As soon as Bredius saw the painting he proclaimed it to be genuine, and in 1938 it was sold to Rotterdam's Boymans Museum for what was then an absolutely enormous sum of money – £58,000 – raised by the Rembrandt Society, various of the city's firms and patrons, and Bredius himself.

Encouraged by his success, van Meegeren painted *The Card Players* and *The Drinking Party* in the style of Pieter de Hooch, both of which he sold for large sums. In the summer of 1939, with the threat of war hanging over Europe, he returned to Holland where he continued to

produce and sell 'Vermeers'. His works from this period include *The Last Supper*, another *Christ at Emmaus*, *Isaac Blessing Jacob*, *The Washing of Christ's Feet*, and *Christ and the Adulteress*. He sold *The Washing of Christ's Feet* to the Rijksmuseum in Amsterdam, and this he considered his greatest achievement and, secretly, his sweetest revenge.

By now, however, Holland was under Nazi occupation and to continue his deception he had to associate with the Germans. Hermann Göring, Marshall of the Reich and art lover, was amongst the most interested in van Meegeren and his 'Vermeers', and in 1941 he traded *Christ and the*

Girl with a Pearl Earring *by Vermeer,* c.*1665, priceless*

*In order to prove that he was not a collaborator, but merely a lovable rogue who had pulled the wool over the Nazi's eyes, van Meegeren had to show that* Christ and the Adulteress *was a forgery. He therefore painted* Young Christ Teaching in the Temple *for the court.*

*In an attempt to make his works look authentic, van Meegeren mixed his own paints to recreate Vermeer's palette and then applied them using brushes made out of badger's hair. He bought up the canvases of lesser known 16th- and 17th-century artists, which he stripped before covering them in his own recreations.*

Adulteress for about 200 paintings that he had bought or looted elsewhere.

When the Allies drove the Nazis out of Holland, van Meegeren found himself in an impossible position. In May 1945 Captain Harry Anderson had discovered *Christ and the Adulteress* in Göring's art collection. Its provenance was traced back to van Meegeren, who was arrested on the very serious charge of collaboration. After two weeks of imprisonment and in order to save himself, on 12 June the artist confessed that he had forged the painting, along with other Vermeers, but at first he was not believed – the story was too fantastic to be credible. The only way he could prove his innocence was to paint another 'Vermeer' specifically for the court. So for two months he was locked in a room with six witnesses and a police guard, where he produced *The Young Christ Teaching in the Temple*. Ironically, this was the first and last direct commission of his entire career as an artist.

After scientific examination of his other works the court was convinced, but van Meegeren was not entirely out of trouble – the charge of collaboration was dropped only to be replaced with one of forgery and fraud. He was by now a national hero, as the sensational story of his exploits became known. Not only had he duped some of the leading experts of the day, but also he had made fools of the Nazis. He was, however, found guilty and on 12 November 1947 he was sentenced to a year in prison. He soon fell ill and despite being transferred to a hospital he died the following month.

We must consider why anyone could be taken in by van Meegeren's fakes. To modern eyes it seems impossible, and yet many dealers, museum curators, connoisseurs and great collectors were completely deceived. One of the main reasons for this was that van Meegeren posed as an expert in Vermeer. He invented an entire 'lost period' for the artist, and hinted that he had access to a cache of undiscovered works from this time. He could then argue that the reason his fakes did not look like other known Vermeers was because they were in a different, unknown style. This is where he was at his most cunning, for if he had copied Vermeer's known style, his fakes would have been clearly apparent. Also, the chaos of World War II made it very difficult to view his paintings and to research the necessary evidence against him. Finally, so many experts had endorsed the fakes that it would have taken great courage to call his bluff.

## Forging Frans Hals

Van Meegeren began his career as a forger by imitating the works of the Flemish artist Frans Hals (1581–1666). In the early 1920s he teamed up with Theo van Wijngaarden to produce a painting called *The Laughing Cavalier*. Van Meegeren produced the work using paint mixed by van Wijngaarden that included gum with the pigment. This meant that the paint would not run when the alcohol test was applied to it. The painting was successfully sold, and the pair continued to produce forgeries such as *Woman Drinking* and *The Poor Wanderer* (below) until *The Laughing Cavalier* was denounced as a forgery by the art expert Dr Bredius. After this the partnership was quickly dissolved.

# TOM KEATING

*The extraordinary thing about Keating is that he manage to fool so many people for so long. He cannot be described as a convincing faker. When you compare this drawing of The Deposition in the manner of Michelangelo to the genuine study for the Lamentation Over the Dead Christ opposite, there can be no doubt that they are by different hands. In his own words, he expressed the ultimate truth: 'If I wanted to be a real faker you would never have heard of me.'*

In 1976 Thomas Patrick Keating hit the headlines when he owned up to having painted a number of fakes over the preceding decade. His extraordinary confessions made him one of the most celebrated forgers of the 20th century.

Originally a house painter, Keating (1917–84) attended evening art classes at Croydon and Camberwell schools. After World War II he won a scholarship to Goldsmith's college, but despite two attempts he failed his diploma. Without the required qualifications he was unable to become an art teacher and so worked as a restorer. Totally disenchanted with the art establishment he

decided on revenge. Claiming to be striking a blow for his impoverished brother artists, he set out to fool the dealers, auctioneers and collectors.

Keating had first made copies of paintings as part of his training whilst at art school and was requested to do others for clients. This eventually led him to start making fakes, or 'Sexton Blakes' as he was fond of calling them. He produced oil paintings, water-colours and drawings in imitation of a huge variety of artists, later admitting to making more than a staggering 2,000 fakes in the style of more than 130 different artists, including Rembrandt, Constable, Degas, Renoir and Turner.

He developed a wide range of techniques to achieve the desired effect. He found old paper and quills for his drawings, and used brown juice from simmering apples and the odd spoonful of instant coffee. He often left clues to his scam within the pictures, the most blatant being to write the word 'FAKE' on the canvas before painting the picture. The writing would therefore be visible should the picture be x-rayed.

The pictures would find their way into the art market, often by way of small country salerooms. For many years he successfully fooled the establishment until an art critic wrote to *The Times* suggesting that a work by Samuel Palmer that had recently been sold for £9,400 was not genuine. The painting was one of 14 'Samuel Palmers' to have been 'discovered' over the previous decade. All had been initially accepted by a variety of respected authorities, but were subsequently discovered to be fakes. Aware he was about to be discovered, Keating wrote to *The Times* to confess his sins. He was sent to trial at the Old Bailey in 1979 for forgery, but the charges were eventually dropped due to his ill health. Keating's resulting fame and popularity with the public led to several biographies, his own television programme, and a Christie's sale devoted to his pictures.

The Deposition *in the manner of Michelangelo by* Tom Keating *(1917–84), £4,000–£5,000*

# Michelangelo

During the Renaissance there was great interest in Greek and Roman works of art, which led to many reproductions of antique marble statues being produced and sold as genuine. Evidence of the seriousness of the situation can be found in a letter sent by the banker Jakob Fugger to his agent in Italy in 1500, in which he tells him to be cautious when buying sculptures for his Antiquarium in Munich. One of the most famous forgers of the period was Michelangelo himself, who as a young student made a copy of a Roman statuette showing Cupid asleep. He sold the work to a cardinal as a genuine antique piece, but then bragged about what he had done. On learning how he had been fooled, the furious cardinal destroyed the statuette. Ironically, had he kept it, it would be worth a small fortune on today's market.

*The strength and sublimity of Michelangelo's creations, the anatomic exactitude and liveliness of his drawings, have been imitated, but never bettered, since his death in 1564.*

Figures Study for the Lamentation Over the Dead
Christ *by Michelangelo (1475–1564), priceless*

# BOOKS AND MANUSCRIPTS

---

The world of paper records the thoughts and ideas of Man, and charts his history back into the mists of antiquity. Fakes abound in this field, but unlike other branches of the fine arts, money is not always the motive – sometimes the perpetrator literally wants to rewrite history. The intelligent eye, coupled with the other senses of touch and occasionally even smell, help the connoisseur rout the deception in ways that we explore through the following examples.

Visitors are often shocked at a *Roadshow* when the expert predicts that the Byron letter he or she is about to be shown is about a vampire, or foretells the wording on a precious message from the king after World War I, but the truth is simple – they are printed copies. The famous vampire letter occurs as the frontispiece to the Galignani edition of Byron's *Works*, but the quality of the printing is so good that it looks like a real letter. The message from George V was an open letter thanking the recipient for his part in defending Great Britain, but it appears to be a personal note on Buckingham Palace headed paper. It was not intended to deceive, on the contrary, it was meant as a personal token to a large number of people. Various politicians and some royalty use this method of thanking people for everything from birthday greetings to Red Cross work.

The great *Hitler Diaries* hoax was meant to deceive, however, and involved a heated debate between historians and manuscript experts over authenticity. Wanting something to be genuine breaks down the first barrier to the fake, which then crosses the credibility gap, and crumbles the power of reason. The popularity and scarcity of material in this and other fields of antiques means the collector must always be wary and question source and substance.

# FAMOUS MANUSCRIPT FORGERIES

There have been many well-documented cases of forgery of manuscripts. William Henry Ireland was one of the most successful with his forgeries of Shakespearean documents. He produced volumes from the Bard's library and other correspondence including a love poem to Ann Hathaway. His success in getting them accepted was his undoing, as he overreached himself with fragments from *Hamlet* and, finally, a new drama *Vortigern and Rowena!* Richard Brinsley Sheridan agreed to produce it at Drury Lane, but as each chapter appeared he became disillusioned and eventually refused to advertise it as being by Shakespeare. Today Ireland forgeries are in great demand.

Another noted forger was 'Major Byron'. Probably born in the USA around 1810, he first turned up in 1843 in Pennsylvania claiming to be Lord Byron's son. His deceit was aided by a remarkable physical resemblance to the poet. He produced many convincing counterfeit letters, not only of Byron, but also of Keats and Shelley,

copying the hands and styles of the Romantic poets with great skill. He was also particularly good at forging postmarks and seals and using the right sort of paper and ink so that even today his work is very hard to detect. He sold his work in England, even managing to sell some to Byron's own publisher, John Murray. Some 19 of his forgeries were published in *The Unpublished Letters of Lord Byron*, which was proclaimed genuine years later by the famous collector (and forger) T.J. Wise (*see pages 98–9*). But when he used an obscure magazine article as the basis for a series of letters 'by' Shelley, Tennyson happened to show these to the son of the author of the article and the forgery was discovered.

The most audacious and prolific forger of the 19th century was the self-educated French peasant Denis Vrain-Lucas. From 1861 he sold to Michael Chasles, a noted mathematician, a collection of forgeries that eventually reached 27,000 letters, manuscripts and documents. The letters were not skilful, and the fraud relied on his ability to gain the confidence of the gullible Chasles. All the forgeries were written in modern French and included letters by Judas Iscariot, Pontius Pilate, Lazarus (before and after his resurrection), Joan of Arc, Dante and Attila the Hun. He was exposed when he forged a letter of Blaise Pascal in which he claimed to have discovered the laws of gravity before Newton. The date of the letter would have made Newton only 10 years old at the time.

Robert Spring was another early forger in the USA, who started in the 1850s forging numerous documents signed by George Washington. The first of these were actually signed on genuine printed forms, which made them difficult to detect. When he ran out of these he wrote the forms in his excellent version of Washington's hand. The strength of his work lay in the lack of hesitation in the handwriting – one of the first

## Forged autographs

In the days of silent movies, Hollywood stars signed their own publicity photos or used a stamp, which was easy to detect. But as the cinema became more popular, the demand for autographs far exceeded the practicalities of personal signing, and studios employed people to sign on behalf of the stars. Unless a signature has been obtained personally it is wise to be careful in this field. The same rule applies to the field of 1960s pop stars. Often fans would hand autograph books in at stage doors and they would reappear with signatures of the Beatles or the Rolling Stones duly in place. In fact, many were signed by assistants.

# Shakespeare signatures

*There are only six examples of Shakespeare's signature that are accepted as genuine, all housed in major institutions.*

*The signatures are all different — even the spelling varies in some cases.*

clues to a forgery is the shakiness that comes from concentrated copying, or where the hand has been raised from the paper mid-composition. Joseph Cosey was the States' most prolific forger, specializing in a range of writers and politicians including Abraham Lincoln and Mark Twain.

## Paper and watermarks

Sometimes forgers make remarkably basic errors, which can be nonetheless easy to miss. Examine the paper on which a letter is written. The earliest documents are almost always written on vellum. Anything that is meant to be pre-Industrial Revolution should be on laid paper and showing a grid pattern of parallel chain lines from the frame on which the paper was made. Wove paper without the grid pattern came into use at the very beginning of the 19th century, often dated in a watermark. A classic forger's mistake is to forget to look at the watermark. A well-written forgery of John F. Kennedy's was made on genuine White House stationery; the forger sadly forgot to hold it up to the light and notice that the watermark was 1981 — 18 years after the assassination.

*The fact that only six signatures exist, and that none of Shakespeare's prolific output is to be found in manuscript, has fuelled the controversy over the authorship of the plays.*

*Conveyance paper of Blackfriars House with William Shakespeare's signature, 10 March 1613, priceless*

# FACSIMILE LETTERS

*July 11th 1911*

Home Office,
Whitehall,
S.W.

*Dear Lord Shuttleworth,*

*My friend Sir William Bailey, of Sale Hall, Cheshire, has written and asked me to support his application for appointment as a Deputy Lieutenant for Lancashire.*

*I enclose the statement of his public services which he has sent me, and if you found it*

*Winston S. Churchill*

*The fact that this letter is addressed to a particular person, and that it is dated, means that it is likely to be handwritten.*

*A letter asking for a personal favour, such as this, is very unlikely to be printed.*

It is a cause of frequent surprise to those attending the *Antiques Roadshow* that convincing facsimiles have been available for over 200 years. Many proud owners of 'original' letters by Lord Byron have been astonished when asked if they are about a vampire. 'How on earth did you know?' Easy really – it is one of the most common facsimiles to turn up.

The original letter was perfectly genuine. When Byron, Shelley, Mary Shelley and Claire Claremont were living at Diodati on Lake Geneva in 1816, Byron had his doctor, William Polidori, with him. On stormy evenings they made up horror stories to amuse each other (Mary later developed hers into *Frankenstein*). Polidori must have made up a story about vampires, as, on his return to England he published *The Vampyre* anonymously, but hinted that it was by Byron to improve sales – an allegation Byron denied. However, Galignani, who published Byron's works in Paris, seems to have mentioned it without the denial. Byron therefore wrote a letter denying authorship on 27th November 1803. It was published in facsimile and included in their one volume *Works* in 1826. It continued to appear in this form in subsequent editions until the last in 1835.

Unfortunately, the facsimile is easily detached from the book and then gets mistaken for the original letter, which has been lost. The first edition facsimile is watermarked C. WISE 1823; later editions have later watermarks or none at all.

Politicians and royalty have also frequently sent out facsimile letters in response to the thousands of letters of congratulation they receive after elections, weddings and birthdays. It would be impossible to answer them all personally, but impolite to ignore them without some token acknowledgement. The most common modern

*Genuine Churchill autograph letter, 1911, £1,000+*

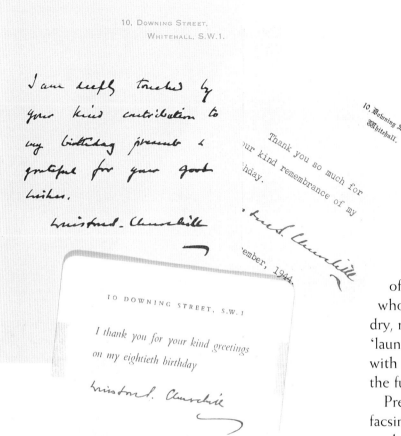

*Generalized thank yous, such as those pictured above, should arouse your suspicions.*

examples are those sent by Sir Winston Churchill. The process is that a suitable letter is written or typed and signed and then printed, and posted to each correspondent.

You can easily distinguish them from their genuine counterparts if you ask yourself three questions. Firstly, is the content consistent with a reply to a letter of admiration? If it is, it could be a facsimile. Secondly, does it have a salutation such as 'Dear Mrs Bloggs'? Facsimiles normally have nothing or 'Dear Sir', which can be added later in another hand. Thirdly, is the date specific, for example, 12th June 1953? (Facsimiles are often

undated, although sometimes a date has been added later.) If the letter is general, unaddressed and undated, then the only possibility of it being genuine is if it was the one that was sent to the printers – unlikely, but possible. Another clue is if a supposedly handwritten letter is sent out in a typed envelope.

Occasionally original documents actually look like facsimiles. Franklin D. Roosevelt and Harry S. Truman signed official documents in very black ink. Roosevelt, whose signatures could take several minutes to dry, referred to his correspondence as his 'laundry'. It was reported that his office was filled with recently signed documents laid out over all the furniture to dry.

Presidents of the United States also had their facsimile signatures engraved on White House cards with a printed message on the back that they were actually reproductions. However, unscrupulous people have been known to get the card split to remove the back. This should be detectable unless it is remarkably well done – if a card is explained as having been glued down into an album and removed you should be suspicious.

Another answer to the pressures of excessive correspondence is the rubber stamp. Stamped signatures have a flat appearance and small white spots can sometimes be detected in both stamped and printed signatures. Woodrow Wilson was the first president to use a typewriter personally, but when governor of New Jersey he often used a stamp to sign the letters he had typed. He gave this up when he became president and took full responsibility for signing his own correspondence. He did continue to type his own letters and was often heard clattering away late at night.

*Facsimile Churchill letters, sentimental value only*

# THE AUTOPEN

The autopen signature is probably the most problematic area of collecting modern autographs. An autopen or signa-signer mechanically produces the exact signature of the writer. The results are not technically forgeries, but they certainly do not have the value of a genuine signature. First of all the writer signs a matrix. The machine 'remembers' this matrix and then reproduces, in biro or even the owner's personal pen, the exact signature. Each 'signature' mirrors the characteristics of the original. The key to identification is in the word 'exact'. No two genuine signatures are perfectly identical, so the only way to spot an autopen is to compare two examples – if they are the same then they are mechanical.

Nearly all presidents of the United States since John F. Kennedy, all congressmen and senators, astronauts, cosmonauts and film stars have employed an autopen to sign their correspondence and souvenir photos. Dwight D. Eisenhower was the last president who did not allow secretaries and machines to sign on his behalf, and even during World War II, when he was Supreme Commander of the Allied Expeditionary Force, he personally signed all his correspondence, though he did allow secretaries to compose some letters for him. Secretaries and machines were used to sign for him during his first presidential campaign in 1952 and again at the end of his life, but with his middle initial omitted.

John F. Kennedy, on the other hand, rarely signed anything himself. Even quite personal photographs with messages of greeting are very commonly secretarially signed. Kennedy started the practice of using several different writing patterns, so that an autopen or secretarial signature was not instantly recognized as such, and this has now become commonplace.

By the time Ronald Reagan became president, the practice was so well-established that even when he handwrote the drafts of letters they were then typed up by his secretary and signed by

*During her reign the Queen has chosen to send informal family portraits as Christmas cards.*

1959.

## Personal messages

Handwritten cards or letters command far greater prices than those signed by an autopen. If a card contains a personal message to the sender, rather than a standard phrase or signature, then it is much more likely to have been handwritten. Such messages, such as the one that appears on this card, which is signed by the Queen using her family name, Lilibet, add a premium to the value of the card.

*Christmas card from the Queen and Prince Philip, handwritten and signed 'Lilibet', 1959, £750*

machine. He even instructed his secretary in the form of signature to use. It is documented that on one occasion he drafted a letter to friends assuring them of his continued accessibility and instructed his secretary to use the machine signature 'Dutch'! Even during his acting career his handwritten letters were sometimes written and signed on his behalf by his mother.

In Britain the autopen is now commonly used by the royal family and politicians. Since 1960 the Queen and Prince Philip have routinely signed their Christmas cards in this way. Considering the quantity that are sent, this is hardly surprising. In the early years they changed the matrix every two years, but it has not changed recently. A good sign to look for is a personal message of greeting, which makes it much more likely to have been genuinely signed. The Prince and Princess of Wales personally signed a lot of cards in the early years of their marriage, but as the pressures of their lives increased these became less common.

Queen Elizabeth, the Queen Mother, has

eschewed the use of an autopen machine to sign her cards, and until a couple of years ago all of her correspondence was genuinely signed – an astonishing feat. The cards sent out by the Queen Mother over the last couple of years have obvious printed signatures.

The values of the cards differ dramatically – an autopen card by the Queen and Prince Philip would sell for about £75, an ordinary one with a genuine signature in the region of £400 and a 'Lilibet' card could top £750. Charles and Diana are more difficult as the value of cards and other material signed by Diana rocketed after her death. They have stabilized now at a much more reasonable level and whereas an autopen card might cost £200 a signed card would probably be between £1,500 and £2,000.

It cannot be stressed too strongly that mechanical signatures can only be reliably identified by comparison with another from the same matrix. It is therefore essential to be sure when buying Royal Christmas cards that whoever you are buying them from knows which are right.

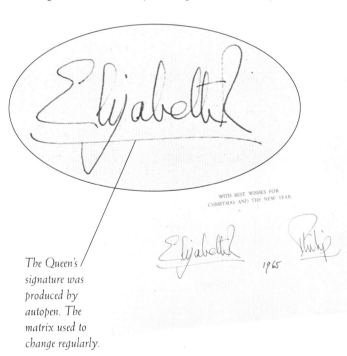

*The Queen's signature was produced by autopen. The matrix used to change regularly.*

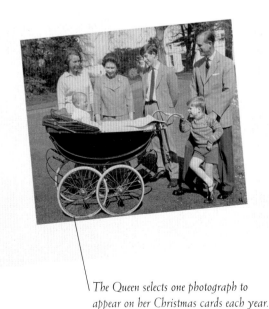

*The Queen selects one photograph to appear on her Christmas cards each year.*

*Christmas card from the Queen and Prince Philip, signed by autopen, 1965, £75*

# THE BOOK FORGERIES OF THOMAS J. WISE

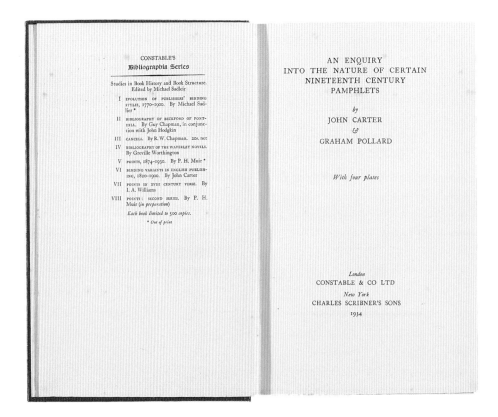

Wise and Forman were exposed as forgers in 1934 when John Carter and Graham Pollard published their research.

Thomas J. Wise (1859–1937) was one of the most remarkable book collectors and forgers of all time. The building of his Ashley Library was the grand passion of his life and he collected Romantic literature with a ferocity that later led to his forgeries. He haunted bookshops and salerooms, and developed a new technique seeking out the friends and families of the authors, for he rightly surmised that they would own association copies that had been annotated by the authors or that had presentation inscriptions. Wise's library was world famous, and in 19th-century authors was considered of 'unapproached completeness'. He was also the author of many bibliographies.

Wise did not forge copies of books already known, which would undoubtedly have led to detection. He forged books that *should* have existed, and who better to decide their titles than someone who knew the authors and their works intimately? For example, there is a well-known story of Elizabeth Barrett Browning handing her husband a bundle of her love sonnets when they were living in Pisa, saying that he should destroy them if he disliked them. Embarrassed, she rushed from the room as he started to read them. Robert Browning recognized the sonnets were remarkable and demanded their publication. To save her feelings they were published as having been translated from the Portuguese in her collected works in 1850. Wise surmised that there should have been an earlier private edition and set about its manufacture. As Wise arranged the printing for the Browning and Shelley Societies, including type facsimiles of rare first editions, the printer was not in the least suspicious about being asked to print an edition of the *Sonnets*, giving 'Reading' as the place of printing and adding 'Not For Publication, 1847'.

The forgeries began around 1882 after Wise met Harry Buxton Forman (1842–1917), a controller of the General Post Office and an expert in printing, and expressed his admiration for his edition of the *Works of Shelley*. In their bibliographical writings, both attempted to legitimize their forgeries. For example, Forman writing about the works of Elizabeth Barrett Browning suggests that it was not the manuscript that she thrust into her husband's hands, but the rare, privately printed Reading edition. Wise knew that Elizabeth's most intimate lady friend at the period when the sonnets were written was Mary Russell Mitford, who lived in Reading. He therefore chose that town for their 'publication', knowing that the experts would assume that she

had arranged it. The pair went on to forge more than 100 works by famous writers, including George Eliot, William Morris, Dante Gabriel Rossetti and Alfred, Lord Tennyson.

Wise and Forman were outed by two brilliant booksellers, John Carter and Graham Pollard, who published a book called *An Enquiry Into The Nature of Certain Nineteenth Century Pamphlets*, in 1934. They found inconsistencies in paper, type, textual inaccuracies, and printing methods. Wise died three years after the publication, never having admitted his part in the frauds, but blaming the already dead Forman. Strangely, on his death, Wise decreed that his Ashley Library should be sold to the British Library. Apart from copies of all his forgeries they found early books made up with leaves from the British Library's own copies! Today, Wise's forgeries are now highly collectable.

## A Stevenson forgery

This pamphlet, which purports to be by Robert Louis Stevenson, is *On the Thermal Influence of Forests*. The printer is said to be Neill and Company, Edinburgh, and it is dated 1873. It was demonstrated to be a forgery by Carter and Pollard in 1934.

*The typeface used – Clay's Long Primer No. 3 – was not cut for the firm until after 1880, seven years after the purported publication date.*

*The cream wove paper is composed of chemical wood, esparto and rag, which could not have been manufactured before 1874 and is highly unlikely before 1883.*

*Wise, T.J. and Forman, H.B. forgery, c. 1883, £250*

# EARLY BOOKBINDINGS

*Studs secured the leather to the boards beneath.*

*Decorating the leather on the finest bindings, usually to portray religious images and heraldic symbols, demanded enormous skill and artistry.*

*Look for signs of wear along the spine – hundreds of years of being opened and closed are bound to leave their mark.*

*Original Italian binding of book of statutes, 14th century*

The handicraft of bookbinding is a traditional art that has changed little over the centuries. Whilst there have been many changes in paper, printing techniques, curing and colouring leather, the leather-bound book is essentially made up of board, leather, thread and glue. In earlier times, it was not uncommon for bookbinders to hold large collections of leather boards salvaged from broken bindings, marbled paper of various dates, and quantities of paper from across the ages. While not wishing to perpetrate a forgery, booksellers would ask their binders to remove poor 19th- or 20th-century bindings on earlier books and ask for contemporary 18th- or 17th-century boards to be added and then a contemporary-style reback. Very often the leather boards would have coronets or crests on them, and some might even have book plates. By attempting to make a better copy of the book, both bookseller and binder were, in effect, deceiving the customer.

There is the case of the London bookbinder who found his work illustrated in the journal of a famous American university where the librarian had gone to great lengths to research the identity of the gilt arms that appeared on the upper and lower boards of a recent acquisition, and drawn conclusions about the previous owner and his 'possession' of the work between those boards.

Louis Hagué, a Belgian bookbinder of great talent and finesse, was working in the late 19th century. His response to the collectors' demands of his age was to elaborately rebind 16th-century books in the style of famous Renaissance collectors. Among these was Diane de Poitiers, the mistress of Henri II of France and a renowned collector of books and fine art. Alan Thomas in his book *Great Books and Book Collectors* (1975, Weidenfeld and Nicholson) remarks 'romantically minded collectors have always been fascinated by Diane de Poitiers, a lady so lacking in consideration for others that she did not leave enough fine bindings to go around'. Hagué proceeded to fill this lacuna. One English collector, John Blacker, was so taken with Hagué's bindings that he collected over 100 of them. He went to his death in blissful ignorance and his executors sent them for sale at Sotheby's, whose description of them as 'A Remarkable Collection of Books in Magnificent Modern Bindings' would have made poor John Blacker spin in his grave.

## Siennese forgeries

In Siena from the 13th to the 16th centuries, the city treasurers produced biannual accounts bound in wooden covers, elaborately decorated in tempera by Siennese artists. They remain for the most part intact in the state archives, but a very few were sold early in the 19th century.

In the late 19th century an artist-gilder named Joni started making them at the suggestion of a dealer. Far from being ashamed of this trade he wrote an autobiography detailing his method.

Having never bothered to visit the state archives to look at them, his examples were again better than the originals, but with additional features not in the originals. Joni sold them at a price too high for a fake and far too low to be original. One angry client, when he found out he had been duped, returned to remonstrate with Joni whose bravura reply to the charge of cheating was 'Yes, but when you bought it, didn't you think you were cheating me?'

# DUST WRAPPERS

*The wear on the spine is equivalent to the wear on the dust wrapper, proving the authenticity.*

*Colour photocopying to a high standard makes reproductions of original designs easier.*

*Check that the paper is authentic to the period of the edition of the book.*

*Well-known authors, whose works command high sums, are more liable to attract the fakers of dust wrappers.*

The Hound of the Baskervilles
*by Arthur Conan Doyle, 1902, £72,000*

The purpose of the dust wrapper on a 'Modern First Edition' was originally to protect the cloth or papered boards from damage on the way from the publisher to the buyer, and they were often discarded after purchase. Dust wrappers certainly existed in the 19th century, although few have survived and much research is still needed into the extent to which they were used. Today, they have evolved into elaborate marketing devices, collectors insist on the presence of dust wrappers, and prices reflect this. There are those in the bookselling world who would argue that the value placed on a dust wrapper is about as relevant to the book inside as collecting 'phone cards is to the conversations that they might once have facilitated. One recent extreme example of wrapper madness concerned a copy of Sir Arthur Conan Doyle's *The Hound of the Baskervilles*, which made over £72,000 at auction with a previously unheard of wrapper. Without the cover, as the book normally appears, the price would have been nearer £2,000.

The incentive to fake wrappers is undoubtedly there, and inevitably with the rise of cheaper and more efficient methods of colour printing and photocopying, and the availability of matching papers, the fake dust wrapper is becoming a pitfall that dealers and collectors alike must be wary of. The dealers' habit, 'all good library practice', of covering the dustjacket with a glassine wrapper often backed with paper for protection, has made the forger's task even easier. The first precaution for the collector is to look for signs of wear. No wear at all is very rare, and can indicate a forgery. The dust wrapper needs examining without its 'protective' wrapper to see if wear, such as it is, corresponds with the book. For example, if the wrapper spine has faded there will be some slight corresponding fading to the book's spine, or dust marking at the top edges will be duplicated on the top edges of the book. Wrappers tend to mould to

and age with their books; they become like gloves over hands, which should make the more simple colour photocopies easy to detect.

Dealers in 'Modern Firsts' are unruffled by photocopy fraud, but confess themselves worried by the 'printed to order' fake. In the wake of the *Hound of the Baskervilles* sale, another copy came on to the market with the same dust wrapper, but on examination the book itself did not look as though it had had the protection of a dust wrapper all its life, and the wrapper – although on the right paper for the period – was too fresh and bore a number of clumsy differences from the original. For those who had not viewed the original, the temptation to accept the fake might have been irresistible, but the giveaways were there.

It is also important for the collector to be aware of the circumstances under which such frauds may be perpetrated. A car-boot sale is too inexpensive a market for such a scam, but an auction, which sells 'as viewed' without guaranteeing what is sold, or a dealer who professes slight knowledge of his or her subject, should be viewed with caution.

## Sherlock Holmes

Since he emerged on to the literary scene in 1887 in *A Study in Scarlet*, Sherlock Holmes has attracted an international following of readers, as well as collectors who feverishly buy all kinds of 'Holmesiana', pushing the prices sky-high. His creator, Sir Arthur Conan Doyle, was aware of their strength of feeling – he lived comfortably on the proceeds of his stories, but was made to feel the wrath of his fans when he tried to kill off the great detective in 1893.

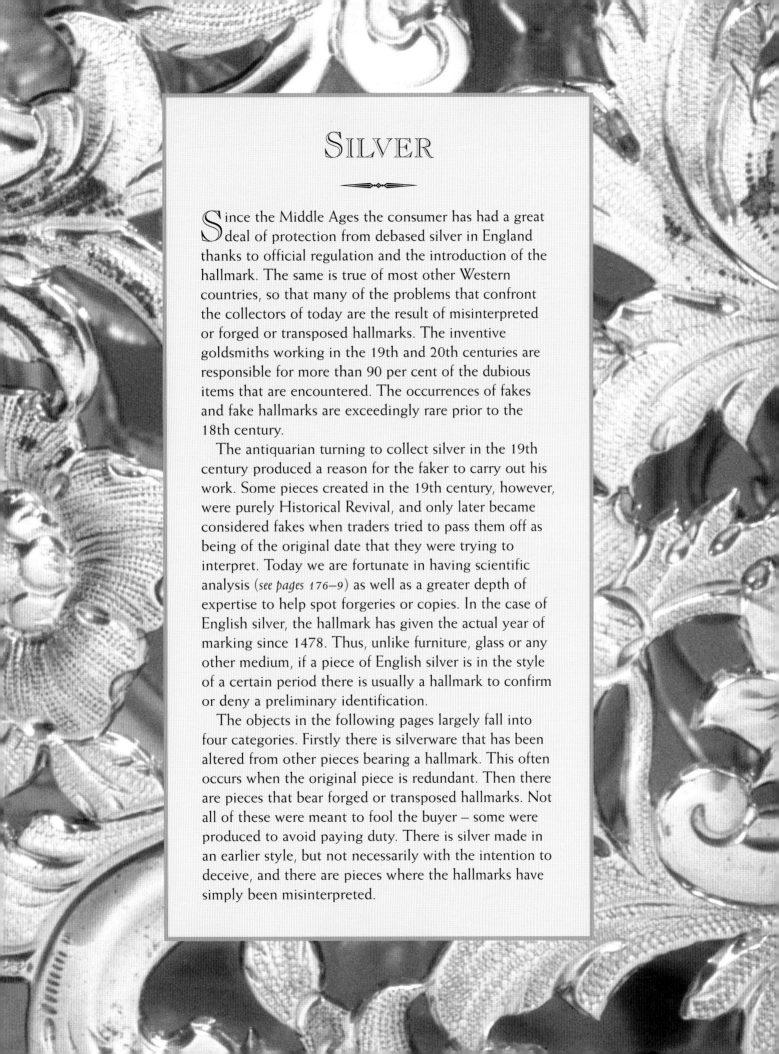

# SILVER

Since the Middle Ages the consumer has had a great deal of protection from debased silver in England thanks to official regulation and the introduction of the hallmark. The same is true of most other Western countries, so that many of the problems that confront the collectors of today are the result of misinterpreted or forged or transposed hallmarks. The inventive goldsmiths working in the 19th and 20th centuries are responsible for more than 90 per cent of the dubious items that are encountered. The occurrences of fakes and fake hallmarks are exceedingly rare prior to the 18th century.

The antiquarian turning to collect silver in the 19th century produced a reason for the faker to carry out his work. Some pieces created in the 19th century, however, were purely Historical Revival, and only later became considered fakes when traders tried to pass them off as being of the original date that they were trying to interpret. Today we are fortunate in having scientific analysis (*see pages 176–9*) as well as a greater depth of expertise to help spot forgeries or copies. In the case of English silver, the hallmark has given the actual year of marking since 1478. Thus, unlike furniture, glass or any other medium, if a piece of English silver is in the style of a certain period there is usually a hallmark to confirm or deny a preliminary identification.

The objects in the following pages largely fall into four categories. Firstly there is silverware that has been altered from other pieces bearing a hallmark. This often occurs when the original piece is redundant. Then there are pieces that bear forged or transposed hallmarks. Not all of these were meant to fool the buyer – some were produced to avoid paying duty. There is silver made in an earlier style, but not necessarily with the intention to deceive, and there are pieces where the hallmarks have simply been misinterpreted.

# METAMORPHOSES

## Wine cup

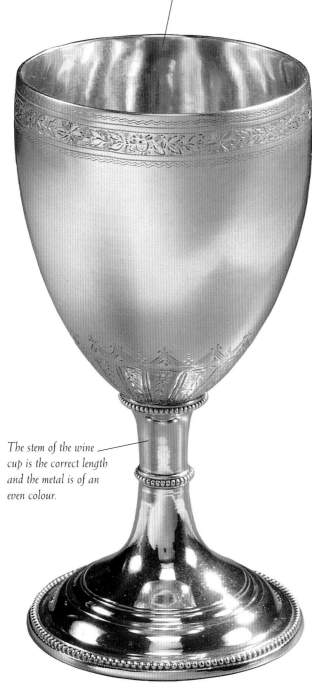

*Silver wine cups or goblets such as this became redundant with the introduction of quality glassware.*

*The stem of the wine cup is the correct length and the metal is of an even colour.*

There are numerous silver objects that have been altered over the past two centuries, either because the originals have become redundant, or simply old-fashioned. Other items have been altered because demand has outstripped supply; thus new pieces have been created to fill the void. The most commonly encountered conversions are drinking vessels turned into serving vessels. It was during the last quarter of the 19th century and the first quarter of the 20th century that most of these conversions were done.

It is important in all cases to look carefully at the balance of the proportions; in original vessels the proportions are harmonious. The construction should also be examined to ensure that there are no more modern techniques used than one would expect. Finally, make sure that the hallmarks are not distorted and that they coincide with a visual dating of the objects.

## Mugs

Thousands of baluster mugs were produced in the Georgian period. The double scroll handle with leaf moulding is the feature that is common to the majority of them and is often the only part of the original that will remain unchanged (*see page 114*). When silver mugs went out of fashion, many were altered into milk or water jugs, usually retaining only the original handle and spreading foot.

Whilst hammering a piece into a different form the metal can become unevenly spread and weak areas need to be reinforced. Often there will be patches let in or applied but these can be difficult to detect if the mug/jug is then decorated with flamboyant chasing, like that on the tankard conversion (*see page 114*). Another form of decoration sometimes used on these conversions is lobing and fluting.

*Wine cup, 18th century,*

*£400*

# Hot-water jug

*A lid and an upper body have been added to turn the wine cup into a water-carrying vessel.*

*The lid should have a lion passant and maker's mark that matches the marks on the base or body.*

*The stem of the original wine cup has been shortened to create the shorter foot expected on a jug.*

*Hot-water jug made from 18th-century wine cup, £150 when re-marked*

# Wine cups

In the late 18th century wine cups were made in fair quantities and these have proved to be readily convertible into small coffee jugs or hot-water jugs. Shortening the stem and adding a lid and upper body are the only major changes that are needed to create these new vessels.

A conversion is not that easy to detect, as the line of the jug is very similar to that of the authentic examples. Look particularly for any changes in colour of the metal and check construction for signs of re-hammering and solder lines in unexpected places. Wine cups are also often converted into milk jugs and wine funnels.

# Plates, dishes and salvers

Dinner services numbering at least 60 dinner plates were an essential requirement for the nobleman or gentleman wishing to take his place in society in the 18th century. The shaped circular plate was standard from 1735 to 1780 and from 1800 onwards. The plain circular plate was popular at other times. These dinner plates were usually accompanied by shaped or plain oval roast meat dishes.

Most alterations or conversions of silver plates are easy to spot because the hallmarks will be partly distorted or missing. It is usually also possible to see creases or seams where the metal has been moved or added to. If the inner edge of the bowl or centre of a circular plate is deeply creased, for example, there is a good chance that an original soup plate has been converted into a dinner plate.

The majority of 18th-century salvers or trays were comparatively plain whilst most 19th-century examples were far more decorative, with floral borders and chasing. As with plates, you should look carefully for hallmarks, creases and seams which suggest re-moulding of the metal.

# Tumbler cups

The tumbler cup, whose heavy rounded base prevented spillage, was a drinking vessel that was popular in the 18th century but gradually fell into disuse. The cups were made in various sizes and the largest were later used as sugar bowls without the need to be altered greatly, except perhaps for the addition of feet. Some smaller versions of tumbler cups have been turned into sugar casters, by adding an upper body and a moulded foot.

Careful examination is needed to detect girdle seams in the conversions, where upper bodies have been added, and there is usually no mark on the cover, as can be seen on the original cup. A lion passant and maker's mark are obligatory for total authenticity. More often than not, however, a poor balance of proportions will give away the conversion as a fake.

# Converted cup

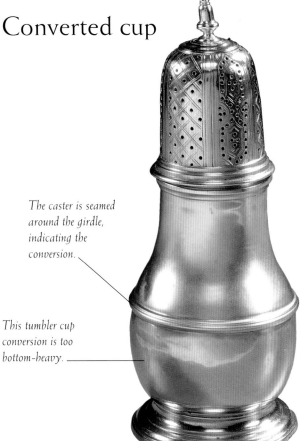

*The caster is seamed around the girdle, indicating the conversion.*

*This tumbler cup conversion is too bottom-heavy.*

*A small example of a tumbler cup has been added to, to make this sugar caster.*

*A 17th-century tumbler cup, so-called because if it is tipped over it will right itself to the vertical again due to its rounded and weighted base.*

*Tumbler cup, late 17th century, £3,500*

*Sugar caster made from an 18th-century tumbler cup, 1730–1900, £100 when re-marked*

# True sugar caster

*Check for a lion passant and makers' mark on the bezel or near the base of the piercing.*

*This original sugar caster has balanced proportions.*

# Pap boot

*This silver pap boat is a small feeding vessel used for serving a mash or pulp of food to infants. Now redundant, many have been converted into cream or sauce boats.*

# Cream or sauce boats

Other pieces of useful silverware that may have begun life as something different are cream or sauce boats. When these have been made from scratch they have an upward curve to the spout, and the feet and handle do not dominate the body. If the proportions of the boat look 'wrong', then it is likely to be a conversion.

Silver pap boats, feeding vessels for young children, were popular between 1750 and 1840. Since that date, conversions into cream boats by the addition of three feet and a scroll handle, or punch ladles made by adding a silver handle socket and a turned wood handle have been more readily saleable objects as collector's items.

Equally, the removal of a silver handle socket and the addition of three feet and a scroll handle can convert the bowl of a punch ladle into a miniature cream boat. These are much less common and the unusual smallness of the body makes them easy to detect. There is also a general awkwardness about the proportions, especially in the lack of balance between the spout and the scroll handle.

*Sugar caster*
*1725, £7,000*

*Pap boat*
*1795, £175*

# Tea caddies and sugar baskets

Tea caddies (from the Malay word *kati*) were a Chinese invention to store their native tea leaves. By the 18th century tea was regularly imported to the West on East Indiamen, and the popularity of the beverage soon surpassed that of coffee. Across Europe and North America silver tea caddies were made to lock away what was to Westerners a new and precious commodity.

In the late 18th century, popularity and demand pushed down the price of tea. Larger caddies became more commonplace and locks became superfluous. The new versions were made out of cheaper materials such as china and wood.

Some original silver tea caddies were converted into related objects, such as teapots, by the addition of a spout and handle, or into sugar or sweetmeat baskets, removing the lid and adding a handle. These conversions replaced a redundant piece with a useful and decorative item.

For information on silver teapots, see page 113.

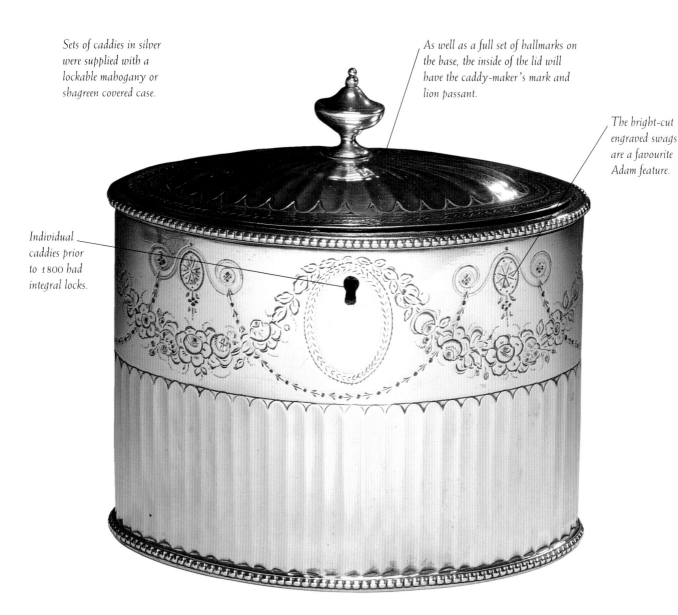

*Sets of caddies in silver were supplied with a lockable mahogany or shagreen covered case.*

*As well as a full set of hallmarks on the base, the inside of the lid will have the caddy-maker's mark and lion passant.*

*The bright-cut engraved swags are a favourite Adam feature.*

*Individual caddies prior to 1800 had integral locks.*

*Tea caddy, 1780, £2,000*

# Sweetmeat basket

*This sweetmeat basket was converted in the 1850s or 1860s from what was originally a tea caddy.*

*With the lid removed and a silver handle added, the conversion from caddy to sugar basket is completed.*

*A lot of work has gone into piercing and embossing the decoration to completely disguise the original caddy.*

## Hallmarks

The sweetmeat basket above should have been re-hallmarked when it was altered in the 19th century. Recently spotted as a conversion, it contravened hallmarking laws. It was sent to the Antique Plate committee at Goldsmiths' Hall, who confirmed the alteration and the original four marks were defaced (bottom left). It was then re-assayed and struck with marks for 1999 and the mark LAO for the London Assay Office.

*Sweetmeat basket converted from 18th-century tea caddy, £120*

# COFFEE POTS

*Coffee pot lids are normally hallmarked on the bezel or inside the dome.*

*The wooden handle was made so that the pot could be held comfortably while containing hot liquids.*

*The line of this original 18th-century coffee pot is elongated and each element is in proportion.*

*The foot rim is light in weight to balance with the main body.*

Coffee, tea and chocolate were all introduced to England in the 17th century and the earliest pots in silver that are normally encountered on the market are 18th century.

The earliest known coffee pot is hallmarked 1681 and is in the collection of the Victoria and Albert Museum, London. Anything marked with an earlier date than that is therefore highly suspicious.

Most 20th-century manufacturers made good replicas of coffee pots and the best are often indistinguishable from the real thing until the piece is carefully examined for constructional differences, colour and patina. The hallmark will, of course, always give the game away. Many reproductions are larger than 18th-century examples, having been made to suit the 20th-century consumption of England's favourite beverage.

Coffee pots are copied and conceived in the style of earlier examples and fake or original marks are then inserted. The most common alterations incorporating hallmarks from another piece are where a tankard has been re-hammered and elongated and then had a spout and finial added. The handle also has to be changed in some way, usually from silver to wood, because a tankard is for cold liquids. The way to spot these conversions is to determine whether the proportions of the piece follow the expected line. Tankards are generally dumpier or squatter and if the line of the body looks disproportionate or unusual in any way, then apply further tests. A tankard will normally have a full set of hallmarks inside the lid, so if you find a full compliment of marks on the lid of a coffee pot you should be suspicious. Coffee pot lids are usually hallmarked with lion passant and maker's mark. In the 19th century there can also be a duty mark and occasionally a date letter.

*Coffee pot, 1734,*
*£3,000*

## Teapots

In the first half of the 18th century tea was very expensive. It was drunk from small tea bowls or cups, less than half the capacity of a modern cup. Early 18th century teapots were also small. However, on occasion, both sugar basins and milk jugs, larger in the 19th century than they are today, were converted into 'rare' bachelor's teapots. Look for a mark or marks on the lid, as without these it's possible that the piece is a conversion. 1780s or 1790s oval teapot stands have been converted, with their original hallmark, to make good replicas, by adding body, lid, handle and spout.

English coffee pots will also be hallmarked in a cluster on the base or on the side of the body in a horizontal straight line to the right of the handle. If you find a pot that has marks in a straight line on the base then it is suspect and is probably a piece known as a 'duty dodger'. These were pieces made in a style that was prevalent between 1719 and 1758, a period when duty payable for assay and marking was 6d (2½ p) per ounce, adding the equivalent of 60 or 70 pence to the cost of an average 25-ounce troy pot. Silversmiths at this time avoided the duty but guaranteed the piece was silver by inserting the marks from some other piece, often an old-fashioned plate or salver that had been handed back to them in part payment of a new purchase. Many makers who did this would stamp their own maker's mark over the maker's mark of the original plate or salver but leave the other three marks in place, making it look as though the piece had been correctly sanctioned for public sale.

Other common pieces to look out for that might be duty dodgers are teapots, two-handled cups, casters and sauce boats. In every case it is essential to check that the marks appear in the correct places and that the style is consistent with the date of the piece.

*The wooden finial on the lid of this reproduction is never found on an original pot of this type.*

*The handle has been simplified at the sockets and the foot rim is slightly heavier.*

*Coffee pot by Messrs Comyns, London, based on an 18th-century design, 1927, £500*

# TANKARDS

The silver tankard or mug is a classic case of an item becoming old-fashioned and redundant. The proliferation of glass manufacturing from the end of the 18th century meant that by the mid-19th century demand for silver drinking vessels had plummeted as glass became the preferred material. It was thus very difficult to sell second-hand examples when they came on to the market.

The result was that many originals were converted into more saleable and useful vessels including jugs, coffee pots, teapots and trophies. The most common conversion is tankard to jug. In fact, such creations had become so commonplace by the end of the 19th century that some manufacturers made replicas of the conversions or fakes!

The two tankards illustrated are very similar in date although the marks on the decorated example have become difficult to read as the chasing has distorted them so badly. The original shape of the converted example is clear, with the alterations being the the added spout and foot extension. The decorative elements are stilted, with the barrel of the tankard having no compatible feel. The handle and thumb piece on the lid are still in their original condition with the exception of added bone fillets in the handle.

*An unblemished example with contemporary armorial and maker's mark of Alice Sheene, London hallmarks for 1709.*

*The double scroll handle with leaf moulding is often the only part of the original that will remain unchanged.*

## Converted tankard

*Handle is almost unmodified.*

*The new spout has been formed with a stiffly cast satyr mask.*

*Embossed and chased decoration of a scene in the manner of Teniers gives the impression of a framed painting.*

*18th century tankard with maker's mark of Alice Sheene, London, £3,000*

*19th century jug made from 18th-century tankard, £1,000 if the additions have been marked*

# 19th-century revival

Impressive decorated silver jugs were made from scratch in the 19th century, so not every jug you will encounter is a conversion. Robert Hennell & Sons produced presentation pieces that were inspired in shape by the 18th-century tankard. The large jug illustrated was made as a retirement gift for a Master of Foxhounds in 1862. The combination of decorative elements in this piece is related by a common theme. There is a clear and careful balance between the foot, body, lid and handle, as well as in the decoration, that is obviously lacking in the converted tankard shown opposite. The designer has worked hard to pull all the elements of construction together to create a balanced decorative piece as well as a useful vessel, as opposed to creating the piece for functionality alone.

## The Britannia standard

Silverware that has had more silver added to it during the conversion process cannot be legally sold in the UK unless the added silver has been submitted for assay and bears an addition mark. This has not happened correctly in the majority of cases. There may be a problem when the original tankard dates between 1697 and 1720. The assay offices of England then had a higher standard of silver than sterling, called Britannia standard. Sterling is 92.5% silver whilst Britannia is 95.8% silver. The reason for the raise in standard was to stop goldsmiths from clipping the edges from coins, thereby debasing the coinage.

The goldsmiths converting pieces in the 19th century nearly always used sterling silver for the additions as Britannia silver had to be specially ordered. The hallmarking act requires all parts of a piece to be a minimum of the standard of the main part. Britannia standard additions can be marked with a sterling additions mark but not vice versa. In the latter case the additions must be replaced with silver of the required standard or the original hallmarks removed.

*A mare and foal finial on the lid.*

*Surreal aspects, such as the dog poking his head out of a tree, are a 19th-century trend.*

*The decoration runs round the body in a continuous flow.*

*Fully genuine jug by Robert Hennell & Sons, 1862, £7,500*

# EARLY SPOONS

Prior to the introduction of French etiquette in dining at the start of the 18th century practically the only item of silver cutlery to exist was the spoon. Spoons were made in their thousands with a variety of different decorative terminals. The most commonly found are the apostle and seal-top spoons, others – including lion sejant, maidenhead and wrythen knop terminals – were rare and few by comparison are found today. The majority of apostle spoons were individual commissions, but some sets of 6 or 12 were made and have survived. The rarest of all is a set of 13 with terminal figures representing Jesus and the 12 Apostles. In the 17th century, plainer spoons were made called slip top, puritan and trefid. By the end of the 18th century, apostle spoons had been out of production for more than 100 years and antiquarians puzzled over why such spoons had been made.

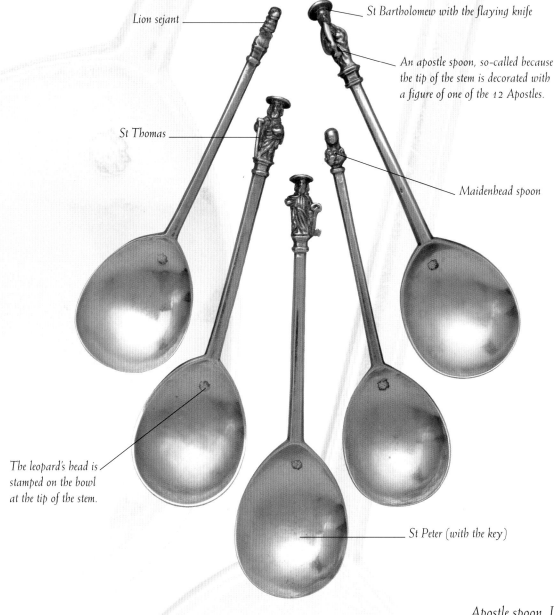

Lion sejant

St Bartholomew with the flaying knife

An apostle spoon, so-called because the tip of the stem is decorated with a figure of one of the 12 Apostles.

St Thomas

Maidenhead spoon

The leopard's head is stamped on the bowl at the tip of the stem.

St Peter (with the key)

*Apostle spoon, London, 1597, £3,500*

# A late 20th-century fake

The high prices gained during the early 1980s for apostle spoons encouraged one particular forger, who managed to fool the market for a year or two. One of his creations is shown on the right. People are usually fooled when they least expect to be. Although the spoon can now be clearly seen as a fake by the experienced eye, at the time many people were taken in.

One of the reasons for this was the material used. Despite modern technology, which uses scientific analysis to help detect forgeries, this recent rogue was clever enough to use silver he had recycled after melting down badly damaged early spoons that had a comparatively low value. He was therefore able to avoid detection longer than he would have done if he had used recently refined metal. He also made an excellent job of the correct constructional aspects, and his 'replicas' were first class. He perhaps tried just too hard to get them right, without having the artistic flare to produce something that would avoid detection for ever. The result is a very 'stiff-looking' product, unlike the more rounded and flowing originals, but to get the hallmarks, construction, patina and metal content so close to the original spoons was nothing short of a stroke of genius.

*St Andrew with saltire cross*

*Each finial was carefully designed to clearly represent the character of one of the 12 Apostles.*

*If genuine, the 'V' joint would have distinguished this spoon as having been made in London.*

*Authentic London spoons too would have a leopard's head mark at the tip of the bowl.*

*The marks are correct for the period – after 1544, London makers placed their maker's mark, date letter and lion passant at the base of the stem.*

*The bowl, like that of authentic apostle spoons, has a pear-shaped flared end.*

*Fake apostle spoon, late 20th century, £20 after remarking – not legally saleable as a fake*

## Victorian interest

Apostle and seal-top spoons were among the most fascinating of all antique silver items for Victorian and early 20th-century collectors. The salesroom correspondent of the *Daily Telegraph* writing about the sale of the 'Tichborne celebrities', as they are now known, went into great detail in both his pre-sale editorial and then his post-sale report on 16th June 1914:

> Tired of the usual terminal figures of the Apostles on christening spoons, an Elizabethan wag of a silversmith was mundane enough to make a set in 1592 with other decorations. He had started in the approved way and had fashioned the Master and St Peter. Then he mildly broke away and designed King David, Joshua and Judas Maccabeus. He next thought of Hector of Troy and Alexander the Great. Still in martial vein he followed with Julius Caesar, Charlemagne, King Arthur and Guy of Warwick, and, as a masterly finish, he adorned the twelfth spoon with a figure of Queen Bess.

The reporter even goes on to quote from Shakespeare's *Henry VIII*: 'Come, come, my lord, you'd spare your spoons'. He also writes '"To be born with a silver spoon in the mouth" is an old proverb illustrating the richness of christening presents'. The spoons eventually sold for £2,000 and he goes on to tell us that a set of 13 Apostle spoons had been bought in 1903 by Mr Astor for the princely sum of £4,900.

These were huge amounts of money and illustrate why 19th-century forgers would try to produce something at that time to get in on the act.

# Later developments

Up to the Restoration, guests would bring their own knife and spoon to a meal, but with the return of Charles II in 1660 Continental eating habits were introduced at Court and spread down through society. Soon, hosts were expected to provide their guests with knives, spoons and, for the first time, forks.

By the turn of the 18th century, the shape of spoons had developed to something fairly similar to that used by diners today. Stems had become much broader and the bowls of the spoons were less fig-shaped.

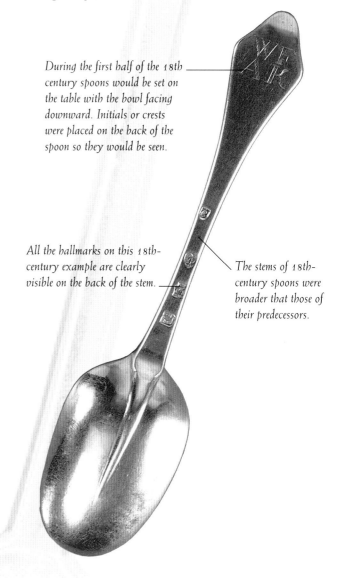

*During the first half of the 18th century spoons would be set on the table with the bowl facing downward. Initials or crests were placed on the back of the spoon so they would be seen.*

*All the hallmarks on this 18th-century example are clearly visible on the back of the stem.*

*The stems of 18th-century spoons were broader that those of their predecessors.*

*Dog-nose spoon, Edinburgh, 1707, £350*

## What to look for

Original London makers fixed the terminals of spoons with a 'V' joint and makers in the provinces with an 'L', or lap, joint. Any deviation from this should be treated with great caution; it may well be that the spoon has been repaired or has had a different terminal put on at a later date. All spoons should be marked in the bowl either with the leopard's head mark or, in the case of provincial spoons, with the maker's mark or town mark. (In contrast to the London spoon, with maker's mark and three assay office marks, provincial spoons are often marked with the goldsmith's mark only. Most often this is punched once in the bowl and then three times on the stem.)

## Fake apostle spoon

The most frequently encountered fake apostle spoons are usually quite easy to detect because they have been converted from 18th-century silver tablespoons, such as the example on the left. These fakes were made in abundance about 100 years ago when collectors were plentiful and supply was scarce. However, design knowledge among the forgers was sketchy, especially in regard to hallmarks and construction. In addition, the casting of the apostle figures was more crude and squat than the elongated versions of the 16th and 17th-centuries.

*Hammering the stem into the thin shape of apostle spoons often distorts the hallmarks.*

*This single spoon has an almost egg-shaped bowl and there is no hallmark struck in the bowl as there are on the original apostle spoons.*

*An original dog-nose spoon has here been converted into an apostle spoon.*

*Fake apostle spoon made from dog-nose spoon, £20 when re-marked*

# SILVER BOWLS

The armorial is hand-engraved and the foot wire is an elaborate feature.

Silver bowls in all sizes from the 17th and 18th centuries have a great appeal to collectors today, but unfortunately very few originals were made and the demand is so great that the market has resorted to creating forgeries, many of which prove hard to detect.

The small bowl, shown opposite, is of nice quality and purported to be made by George Wickes. It also has a hallmark that appears to be 1735, on the face of it a valuable piece for its size (5¼ in diameter, 8¼ troy ounces in weight). But the marks are not very clear, despite being on the underside where the piece would not normally get any wear. Looking at the bowl shown on the left, which has a genuine 1735 hallmark, there are sufficient differences to support the theory that the first bowl is a recent reproduction. All the edges of the marks on the fake bowl are much more blurred than on the original, and the leopard's head, date letter V and the lion passant do not follow the correct design requirements as seen on the genuine hallmarks, (below left). The GW mark is also too squat and more poorly formed than the genuine Wickes mark. Other notable differences are the blurred armorial and the over-simplified foot wire. When the silver was analysed at Goldsmiths' Hall, it was also found to be modern silver. Although at first the piece appears to be genuine, it is fairly easy to spot the tell-tale differences from the original if time is taken to study the above features.

The Goldsmiths' Hall try to make sure that such pieces have their offending fake marks removed. It is illegal for the forgery to be offered for sale and if that happens the Goldsmiths' Hall and the Trading Standards Office have the power to seize the offending articles. When The Antique Plate Committee has confirmed the piece as a fake, the owner has the choice of having the piece back with the marks defaced and then having the

In an original, the lion passant's tail curves over his back, rather than touching the head as on the reproduction.

The right-hand stroke of the 'V' should be thinner than the left-hand stroke, as shown here, and not of equal weight.

The crowned leopard's head on original 18th-century bowls is far slimmer around the cheeks than it is on the reproduction.

*Sugar bowl, 1735*
*£1,500*

piece assayed and marked with the silver and year marks of the time that it is submitted.

The small rose bowl or presentation bowl was very much in vogue between 1875 and 1930, so reproductions were rife to satisfy demand and deceive the purchaser. To detect a fake, look at the placing and detail of the hallmark. Original bowls are more often than not marked on the underside between 1720 and the late 18th century, but on the side of the body before 1720 and after 1800. Most of the late 19th-century forgers, hammering up bowls from old silver plates or letting-in marks, made the mistake of placing 18th-century marks on the side of the body. The largest bowls will also usually have a more substantial spreading foot.

*When compared with genuine 1735 hallmarks (see left), the marks on the fake silver bowl are blurred and have obvious stylistic differences.*

# Fake silver bowl

*The armorial is worn in an uneven manner and looks as though it has been acid etched.*

*The simple foot wire, shown here, is unlike anything you would normally expect from bowls produced at this particular date.*

*Bowl, dated 1735 but actually modern forgery, £200 when re-marked*

# ROCOCO SOUP TUREEN

The most innovative time in the development of silver design and quality craftsmanship was the age of Rococo style, which incorporated excessive ornamental details often superfluous to the function of the object.

French silversmiths were at the forefront of the new age in the first and second quarters of the 18th century. Juste-Aurèle Meissonnier inspired future generations in the art of asymmetrical creations, but perhaps the most admired and best known of all French goldsmiths was Thomas Germain. His work encompassed superb sculptural detail and creativity of design without ever losing the delicate balance that eluded many of his contemporaries. When the silver soup tureen, cover and stand illustrated below was made by Germain in Paris in 1733–4, it became an icon of its age. The fine finish and complexity of detail

surpasses any other contemporary tureen cast in silver. The abundance of the decoration all over the body and the diversity of the assembled elements are magnificently incorporated to create a beautiful but balanced work. Fit for the king's table at a time when dining was a wonderfully theatrical and ceremonious event, it was no doubt commissioned by an extremely wealthy patron. Indeed, the tureen was in the possession of the French royal family during the second half of the 18th century. The silver used is of very high standard with less than 5 per cent of alloy.

During the following three decades elaborate soup tureens continued to be made, such as the example illustrated opposite by Christian Drentwett II, Augsburg, 1763–5. Here, however, it can be seen that the decoration has become much more restrained, with simpler foliage decoration

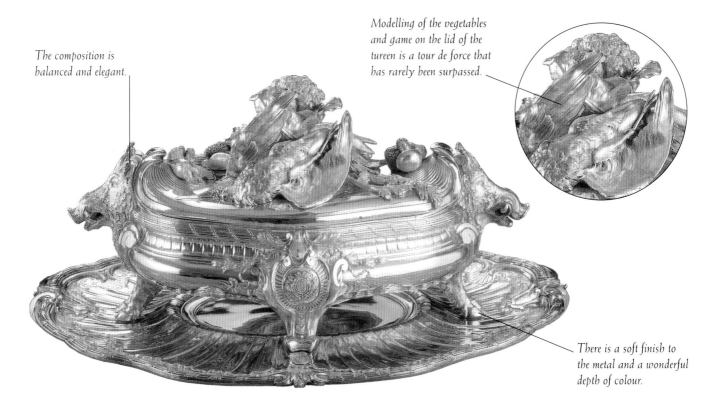

*The composition is balanced and elegant.*

*Modelling of the vegetables and game on the lid of the tureen is a tour de force that has rarely been surpassed.*

*There is a soft finish to the metal and a wonderful depth of colour.*

*Rococo soup tureen, cover and stand by Thomas Germain, 1733–34, £6,000,000*

around the borders and feeble depictions of vegetables when compared to those of the Thomas Germain tureen. There is also less cast work added to a more basic, smooth oval shape and the composition has become more symmetrical. The piece would have been a fraction of the cost of the masterwork, and therefore able to be sold on a much wider scale.

In the 19th century silver manufacturers had the opportunity to create elaborate designs at an even lower cost. Replicas were made of 18th-century designs and some of these are almost indistinguishable from the originals without close observation and examination of the marks.

Most pieces by this time, however, were created using a very thin gauge of silver making them quite easily distinguishable from original Rococo tureens. The handles and feet were cast in the traditional way, albeit with less silver than on an 18th-century piece, but the sides would have been stamped out in sections in huge metal dies and then assembled and hand-finished. Jardinères are open in the base and an inexpensive metal liner made of tin or a gilded copper alloy is supplied to fit. The amount of silver involved is about a quarter of that used in the smaller Drentwett piece. Many manufacturers also used silver with 20 per cent alloy thus reducing the cost even further.

*Decoration became much less flamboyant during the second half of the 18th century.*

## Extravagant dining

During the 18th century, candlelight, mirrors, fabrics and perfumes were all used to heighten the senses of diners to the array of food and delicacies put before them. Debates on flavours and recipes abounded in Court circles, and the enthusiasm for food and new dishes was greater than it is even today.

# 19th-century jardinière

*Vegetable dishes or jardinières were often based on Rococo designs. This example is light in weight, with openwork elements giving an airy overall effect.*

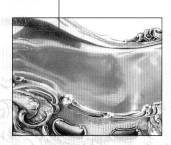

*Soup tureen, cover and stand by Christian Drentwett II, 1763–5, £26,000*

*Jardinière by Bruckmann & Sohne, c. 1880, £5,000*

# NUREMBERG BEAKERS

The silver-gilt beaker (*left*), engraved with biblical scenes, is of a type that was popular in Germany during the 16th and 17th centuries. Such beakers are occasionally referred to as *Monatsbecher* ('*Monat*' being the German word for 'month', '*Becher*' for 'beaker'), as they were often made in sets of 12 and were decorated with symbols representative of the months or the signs of the zodiac.

There are some very good 19th-century copies in existence that need careful examination to assess whether or not they are really what they are claiming to be. The balance of the decorative elements is very important when trying to separate original from reproduction. The engraved work on 16th-century German beakers usually has a wonderful freehand quality. Many engravings were inspired by prints, but tend to be interpretations that showcase the engraver's own artistic talent rather than methodical copies. Replicas dating from the 19th century, even those made by the finest goldsmiths, often have stiff and stilted engraving that can be clearly seen when one is placed next to the other.

It is sometimes difficult to establish where a 16th-century beaker was made, as workshops would exchange and share patterns as a matter of routine. Often there is very little difference in the overall result between two beakers made at separate workshops. In detail, however, minute differences in the finish can be spotted, where castings have had to be cleaned off and the design has been hand-chased to improve the clarity of the ornament.

The four beakers (*right*) are English replicas of a set of four by Eustachius Hohman of Nuremberg, and were made by Rundell, Bridge & Rundell, the royal goldsmiths in London in 1827. The beakers' proportions have been slightly elongated in comparison with the originals, but the quality and

Silver and other metals have been used for making lasting drinking vessels since the earliest times of civilization. The British Museum recently acquired a remarkable Roman gold drinking cup, which is decorated with scenes of male lovers. There has been some press speculation about the cup's authenticity – some believing that it dates from a later period – but, as with all objects, authenticity comes down to the correct description. Good designs are naturally copied and replicas can sometimes sell for as much as the originals.

## Augsburg beakers

Another popular design of German beaker was that embossed with profile portraits of Roman emperors. They were made in the later part of the 17th century and in the early 18th century. Again the original is quite broad and squat (*right*) and the portraits dominate the decoration. This example by Cornelius Poppe was made in Augsburg, *circa* 1685. They are often also chased with trophies of war and usually parcel gilt with the portrait left white and the surround gilded. This example has been re-gilded which affects its value and can be disturbing to the eye when testing authenticity.

The copy (*left*) is a really rogue item: not only has the silversmith got completely the wrong shape, he has also gone for the wrong country of origin. The tall flared shape is more akin to 16th-century Scandinavian and Netherlandish designs. The base has hallmarks for London, 1749, and the piece was doubtless made from a plain beaker or mug. The portrait is dominated by the foliate chasing instead of the other way round. Probably made towards the end of the 19th century, this type of item took up the demand for antique plate created by the Rothschilds and other great collectors whose appetite for such pieces seems to have been insatiable.

## 19th century replicas

finish are equally good. The rims and the bases have been taken from castings of the 16th-century beakers and are extremely close to the original interpretations. The engraved tassel work has been completed with little feeling, however, and does not have a realistic look. Rather it gives the appearance of having been carefully copied in draughtsman-like fashion.

The firm of Rundell, Bridge & Rundell was — through great collectors such as the Duke of York and William Beckford, and its designers John Flaxman and Augustus Pugin — an important participant in the early 19th-century Antiquarian movement. In 1808, for example, the firm took a quantity of Royal Plate in part payment for new commissions from the Prince Regent. Instead of melting the items down they were sold on as antique plate.

*These 19th-century examples are deeper than their German predecessors.*

*The beakers' rims have been cast from 16th-century originals.*

*The engraving, although of the finest quality, does not have the spontaneity of earlier works.*

*Set of four beakers by Rundell, Bridge & Rundell, London, 1827, £18,000*

# PRECIOUS OBJECTS

◆━━◆━━◆

Jewellery, like just about everything else, has been copied, forged or faked over the centuries although infinitely more acceptable terms, such as 'enhanced' or 'improved' are used to mitigate what is a clear intention to deceive. As early as the 14th century, gems were shown to their best advantage by placing a piece of coloured foil between the stone and setting. Regulations were introduced to try and prevent this from happening, but the problem remained fairly widespread. Another technique called 'flashing' involved layers of coloured and colourless glass being combined to produce an effect similar to the appearance of ruby and sapphire. Today, we can only guess at how the public must have been taken in by counterfeit products of this sort.

In the 17th century, importation of imitation stones and false pearls reached near epidemic proportions, until Charles I issued a proclamation threatening forfeiture and loss of property for those persons found guilty of wearing or trading the goods. By the 1700s, pastes copied diamonds, pinchbeck took the place of gold, and gemstones were often foiled to 'improve' their colour.

The 19th-century goldsmiths 'revived' the styles of the Ancient Egyptians, Etruscans and Assyrians, often using ancient hardstones and coins, whilst the opulence of the High Renaissance was replicated throughout Europe in tasteful (and tasteless) facsimiles, set with gems and curiously shaped baroque pearls.

The jewellery of the 20th century has seen fakes of many of the most famous manufacturers. Gemstones such as emeralds are treated with oils and resins to enhance their colour, and diamonds are irradiated to transform an ordinary stone into a fancy blue, yellow or pink. The prized jewels of the 1920s and 1930s are reproduced by the score in ever more sophisticated settings and even humble gold seals are copied in 9 carat gold to give the appearance of the genuine article.

# RENAISSANCE PENDANT

The intricacy of the carving on the cameo is exceptional.

The pendant has simple table-cut rubies and diamonds and strong polychrome enamelling.

The pearl was an indicator of status, worn by all who could afford them.

The explosion of cultural and artistic changes that took place in 16th-century Europe had a huge impact upon jewellery design and manufacture. Starting in Italy, and quickly spreading to Spain, Germany, France and England, the master jewellery-goldsmiths such as Benvenuto Cellini and Virgil Solis created sophisticated and intricate necklaces, pendants, hat badges and reliquary crosses enriched with polychrome enamels, pearls, rock crystal, rubies and diamonds, imported by way of the newly established trade routes.

The pendant was particularly popular and amongst some of the most beautiful designs of the period were animals with pearl bodies, ships with finely wrought hulls, birds with enamel plumage and mermaids with iridescent tails studded with gems, all manufactured for merchants and nobility.

The Renaissance jewel displayed wealth and power. Queen Elizabeth I employed many artists to immortalize her image in media such as hardstone cameo, and Nicholas Hilliard, the court miniaturist, painted his queen's portrait to mount within a sumptuous jewel that was presented by a grateful nation to Sir Francis Drake. The Drake Jewel is set in the centre with a double hardstone cameo of a blackamoor and classical goddess in a ruby and enamel frame with an egg-shaped pearl suspended below, creating one of the finest examples of splendour from the High Renaissance.

During the 17th century fashion gradually gave way to lighter, subtler designs in line with greater understanding of gem-cutting and setting. By the 18th century the diamond was in universal demand, inspiring a glittering array of jewels in the form of bows, clusters, sprays, wreaths and flowers, faithful in their conception.

The growth of the middle classes created by the Industrial Revolution meant that by the 19th century the diversity and volume of jewellery being produced was staggering. All over Europe

*The Drake Jewel, front and back,*
c. 1580, *priceless*

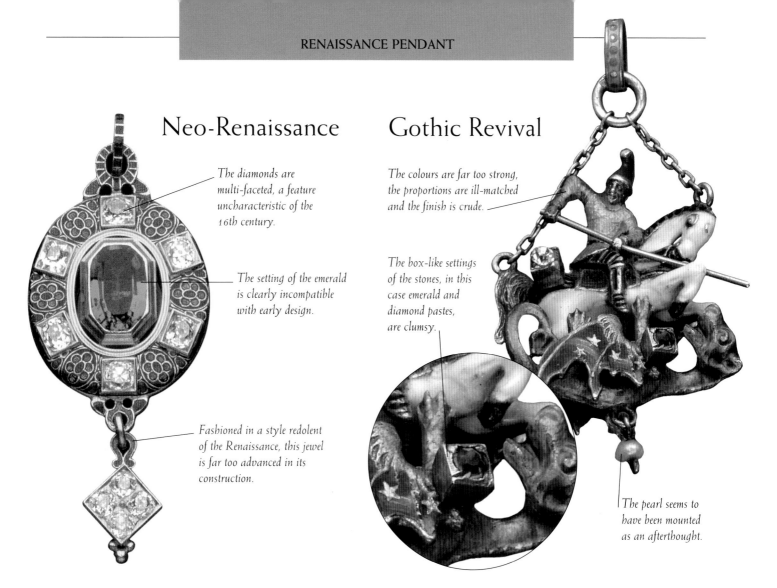

# Neo-Renaissance

*The diamonds are multi-faceted, a feature uncharacteristic of the 16th century.*

*The setting of the emerald is clearly incompatible with early design.*

*Fashioned in a style redolent of the Renaissance, this jewel is far too advanced in its construction.*

# Gothic Revival

*The colours are far too strong, the proportions are ill-matched and the finish is crude.*

*The box-like settings of the stones, in this case emerald and diamond pastes, are clumsy.*

*The pearl seems to have been mounted as an afterthought.*

the newly rich had sufficient disposable income to be able to afford jewels, and craftsmen such as Carlo Giuliano, Castellani and John Brogden caught on to the fascination with the past by manufacturing gold, enamel and gem-set pieces in the Archaeological Revivalist taste; necklaces, pendants, brooches and bracelets often used ancient hardstones such as agate and lapis lazuli.

In 1834 a Tudor-Gothic style was chosen for the Houses of Parliament in London, which led to a revival in Gothic and Renaissance design in English jewellery. In Paris, Francois Desirée Froment-Meurice designed a Gothic silver bracelet which was shown at the 1851 Great Exhibition in London, and in 1855 he exhibited two St George and the Dragon pendants in Paris. By the 1870s, French goldsmiths were making pieces in the Neo-

Renaissance style, faithfully representing the designs of the 16th-century artist Hans Holbein. Mounted at the centre with a precious gem, or more frequently a garnet cut *en cabochon*, the frames were *champlevé* enamelled in blue, red and green, studded with diamonds or green chrysolites and chased with scroll decoration on the reverse. Some Neo-Renaissance jewels were so plausible that they were sold as 16th-century examples.

The fashion continued into the 20th century, spawning the far cruder execution of gem-set and enamel pieces in Eastern Europe. They were usually made in silver, sometimes set with pearls, garnets or foiled emeralds, and often enamelled in livid shades. They bear little relationship to the splendour or delicacy of the past, but still reflect Gothic Revivalist themes of the period.

*Holbeinesque emerald, enamel and diamond Neo-Renaissance pendant, c.1870, £15,000–£20,000*

*Eastern European pendant, c.1900, £150–£200*

# Diamond Jewellery

## The cut of a diamond

The way that diamonds are cut has changed over the years. Old mine-cut diamonds were used throughout the 19th century, but were often remounted during the Edwardian and Art Deco periods. Round-cut brilliant diamonds were in vogue from 1900 to the late 1930s, after which time they were replaced by modern-cut diamonds.

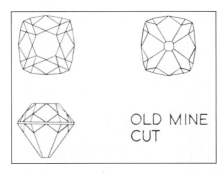

OLD MINE CUT

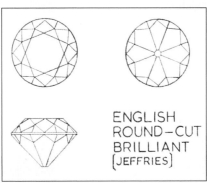

ENGLISH ROUND–CUT BRILLIANT (JEFFRIES)

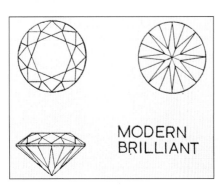

MODERN BRILLIANT

It is very important today to be able to distinguish between old and reproduction jewellery. In most cases, genuinely old pieces will tend to be much more valuable than their reproductions. The substantially greater value and collectibility of old pieces gives an incentive to deceive, whether knowingly or unknowingly.

The periods most often reproduced are those in greatest demand. At the time of writing, the taste is for the very finely made pieces of the Edwardian (1900 – 1920) and Art Deco (1920 – 1940) periods. The very colourful designs associated with the Art Deco period are foreshadowed by pieces produced as early as 1910 by Cartier and other French ateliers, whereas the main keynote of the Edwardian style is absence of colour, 'high'

*The setting holes have been opened out and shaped to give the piece a light, delicate feel.*

*The back of this diamond encrusted Art Deco bow brooch reveals round-cut diamonds that are in keeping with the period. The diamonds are set in platinum, which was the favoured metal for jewellery of such quality.*

*An Art Deco diamond and platinum bow brooch*

jewellery being characterized by the almost exclusive use of diamonds and/or pearls.

The Edwardian style conveniently coincides with the general replacement of silver by platinum in diamond jewellery. Platinum is extremely hard and strong, allowing jewellers to produce delicate saw-pierced lacy settings. From this point onwards, until the late 1930s, all good quality diamond jewellery was set in platinum, and only cheaper ranges were produced in white gold, which is much softer.

One of the first indications as to whether a piece is old or new is the cut of the diamonds. The brilliant cut was introduced as early as the late 17th century, but was progressively refined. Earlier stones were cut to retain more of the weight of the rough and did not, as with modern-cut stones, come to a point at the bottom, but terminated in a small cut-off extra facet. Towards 1900 it became more normal for diamonds to be cut with a round outline, and throughout the first half of the 20th century, scientific calculations resulted in cuts that showed the fire and dispersion of brilliant-cut diamonds to the best effect. Briefly, the depth above and below the girdle, or perimeter, of the stone decreased, and the table became bigger. It was not until the end of the Art Deco period that diamonds began to be cut to a point at the bottom. It was also quite common for Georgian and Victorian pieces to be broken up and re-set in the current fashions, so stones of an earlier cut are frequently found in Edwardian or Art Deco pieces. What you do not find are modern-cut pointed stones, which did not come in until the very end of the Art Deco period. Modern-cut stones and their settings can be highly uniform, especially the many small stones that are largely now machine-cut.

With most old pieces, the back is as informative as the front, and this is especially true of jewellery,

which tended then to be made for wealthy and discerning clients who knew the appearance of good finishing. When you examine the back of an old piece of good quality, you will see that the stone holes are not simply left round as drilled, but are carefully shaped with needle files into hexagons, squares or triangles, the idea being to remove as much metal as possible, so giving an extremely light effect.

If by comparison, you look at most reproduction jewellery, a lot of the settings are cast; the black holes are left in the round, or crudely shaped; and the backs of the settings will have a slightly uneven look because they have not been carefully filed. The majority of pieces will be set in white gold rather than platinum.

*If the back is examined under a loupe then the poor quality of the finishing is revealed.*

*This bracelet is a modern reproduction of an Art Deco design, perhaps taken from one of the many books on jewellery of this period that are currently on the market.*

*Modern reproduction of an Art Deco bracelet*

# FABERGÉ OBJET D'ART

*This fine quality Fabergé powder compact bears the marks of the house and workmaster as well as the assay mark for St Petersburg 1908–17 and a scratched inventory number. It is also illustrated in the original design book, which dates to 1911.*

In the illusory world of fakes and forgeries, there is one discipline that seems to stand out for the sheer volume of counterfeits produced and the relentlessness with which they are proffered as the genuine article. Literally thousands of spurious Fabergé objects exist in the world today – some extremely plausible and some downright atrocious – and their number has risen in direct proportion to the astronomical prices achieved by Fabergé *objets*.

Everyone would like to own a piece of Fabergé; the designs are exquisite, the enamelling and gold work is incomparable and the hardstones are voluptuous. However, our desire for Fabergé is, perhaps, more deeply seated and intangible. Owning Fabergé means possessing an object of pre-Revolution Russian history. The Tsar himself patronized Fabergé and the tragic and awful events of that time undoubtedly add an extremely potent ingredient to the overall desirability of the subject matter itself.

The opportunity to forge Fabergé was made all the more easy by the rigid Russian hallmarking regulations, which stated that any gold or silver item had to bear the necessary identifying 'punches' provided there was sufficient space available on the object itself. However, if the object was too small or delicate, the necessity for hallmarking could be waived. The additional fact that no law existed in Russia to make hallmarking platinum compulsory resulted in an ideal environment for forgers to flourish and so, if a piece of platinum jewellery bore no identifying marks, who could prove that it was not by Fabergé? The problem was compounded by the fact that Fabergé did not engrave his hardstone animals or carvings with an identifying mark, offering the forgers limitless scope for highly profitable counterfeiting.

*The diamonds or gems on a piece of Fabergé should be of the finest quality and their cut should be consistent with the period of the piece (see page 130).*

*The uniformity of colour, its depth, its patina and finish, mean that Fabergé enamels are truly incomparable.*

*Face powder compact by Fabergé, £15,000–£20,000*

Faking Fabergé was already becoming a problem by the 1930s, and by the 1950s the 'industry' was expanding in line with sharply rising prices and more sophisticated production. This led to flower studies, photograph frames, hardstone animals and gem-set jewellery being regularly 'discovered' in the United States, Germany and even Russia itself. Generally speaking, these fakes were facsimiles of genuine objects and were fairly easy to spot. By the 1960s, however, authentic Russian artefacts surfaced bearing cleverly superimposed Fabergé hallmarks and hardstone carvings started to appear at auction, often with very plausible provenances. The problem was further exacerbated by a gullible and greedy public desperate to own a piece of Fabergé. In this fertile climate, the forgers were able to sell some absolutely appalling copies for large amounts of money.

*This straightforward (and badly repaired) Victorian diamond flower spray brooch has been ennobled by the addition of several fake Fabergé hallmarks. These marks are inconsistent with an item that is clearly not of Fabergé style or quality.*

Today, the forgeries are far superior and many Fabergé fakes are, frankly, extremely difficult to identify. However, no matter how sophisticated the fake may be, it can never quite achieve the supreme technical mastery of the genuine article.

If you are offered a piece of Fabergé and you are not sure if it is genuine, look at the quality of the enamelling and the cut of the gemstones. If it is a hardstone animal, then check for signs of a unique personality and humour – fakes lack the essential Fabergé individuality and quality of carving. Be wary of over-plausible documentation if the item is modestly priced.

If the piece is in a presentation box, check the quality of the wood – Fabergé used lovely Russian woods, most frequently hollywood and sometimes Karelian birch and oak. Fakes are often badly finished, can be stamped with inaccurate house marks in the lids and use uncharacteristic material for the blocking on which the object resides.

Finally, should you be considering investing thousands of pounds in a Fabergé *objet d'art*, seek the opinion of an acknowledged expert at one of the leading shops, auction houses or museums.

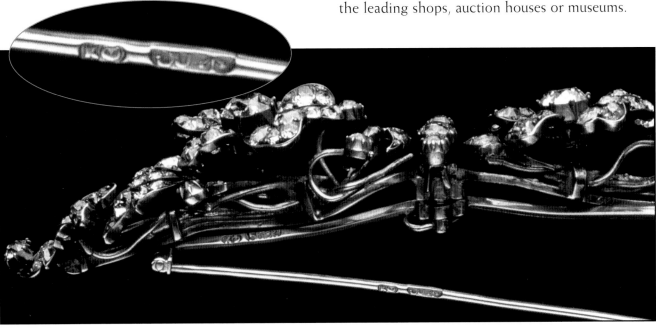

*Diamond flower spray brooch with fake Fabergé hallmarks, Victorian, £45,000 due to value of stones*

# PASTE

*This 18th-century silver brooch is set with a combination of brown and colourless pastes.*

*The open-backed style of jewellery popular in the 18th century was perfectly suited to pastes.*

Glass as a substitute for gemstones has been used in decorative ornamentation since ancient times. It was not until the 18th century, however, that glass as a highly adaptable medium for use in jewellery really took off in popularity. The primary reason for its success in Europe was the development of gem-cutting as an art and the gradual progression from solid, closed-back mounts to the lighter, more versatile open-backed kind of setting.

The glass compound invented to imitate precious stones was known as paste, and it was largely developed in the 1730s by Georges-Frederic Strass, a Frenchman, who found that the addition of certain oxides and crystals to flint glass resulted in a material that was sufficiently hard to cut and polish in a similar way to gemstones. The diversity of colour and high degree of brilliance obtained meant that all the known gemstones could be copied cheaply and effectively and set in an all-embracing array of designs. Like many new materials, paste was seen as new and exciting when it first hit the market.

*Tiaras such as this one are currently very fashionable and so command high prices.*

*At the beginning of the 19th century paste jewellery that displayed a high degree of workmanship was still being produced.*

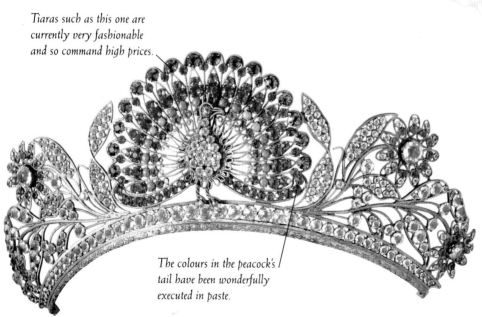

*The colours in the peacock's tail have been wonderfully executed in paste.*

*ABOVE: An English peacock tiara set with coloured and colourless pastes, early 19th-century, £2,000–£3,000.*

*TOP LEFT: A silver brooch with brown and colourless pastes, 18th-century, £1,000–£1,500*

Paste jewellery quickly became popular throughout Europe and was a huge commercial success due to the fact that it had the appearance and all the social acceptability of the genuine article at a fraction of the price. Today, 18th-century paste jewellery is in high demand due to its beauty and rarity, and a 'Queen Anne' necklace made up of paste sections can fetch £2,000–£3,000 at auction. More modest brooches and earrings of the period are worth £200–£1,500 depending on the size and quality of the workmanship.

The quality of paste jewellery deteriorated during the 19th century, primarily because the open-style settings were inappropriate and also because the Victorians regarded paste purely as imitation. Towards the end of the century, French jewellers produced pretty pendants and necklaces suggestive of the sinuous lines of the rapidly emerging Art Nouveau taste, but the paste itself was often poorly set and rather glittery. It was quite common for paste of this period to be foiled to enhance the colour or show off the glass. Even then, however, the charm and beauty of the 18th-century material was missing.

By the 1920s and 1930s, the fashion for glamourous and colourful jewels inevitably led to a demand for affordable copies, and the designs of firms such as Cartier, Boucheron and Tiffany were faithfully copied in paste and sold to the general public. In the United States, Miriam Haskell designed daring and highly original costume jewels with a particular emphasis upon colour co-ordination and wearablilty and in Europe, couturiers such as Dior, Schiaparelli and Chanel produced innovative and exciting jewellery to complement their costume creations. Today a Dior necklace or Haskell bracelet can fetch several hundred pounds, representing an area of steady growth in an important medium that stretches back 300 years.

*Art Deco diamond jewellery was imitated in paste for those who wanted to wear fashionable accessories but who did not have the bank balance to match. This is a direct copy of a diamond double clip.*

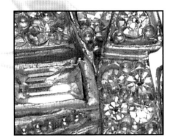

*The pastes in this brooch are foil-backed to enhance their shine and are set in a chrome-plated metalwork mount.*

## Paste or gem?

Certain tests help to distinguish between real gems and paste. Firstly, due to its low heat conductivity, paste feels warmer to the touch than most gemstones. Secondly, paste is fairly soft and therefore reveals chips and abrasions to the surface facets – gemstones are considerably harder and less prone to damage. Thirdly, upon examination under a lens, paste frequently contains bubbles and swirl marks, whilst real gems tend to contain natural crystals and characteristic inclusions, and finally, early paste were frequently mounted in low-grade domed metal backs.

*An Art Deco brooch set with foil-backed pastes in a chrome plated metalwork mount, c. 1935, £25–£75*

# COLLECTABLES

The time when you have to break the news to the owner of an object that what they hold is nothing more than a clever fake is one of the toughest moments in an *Antiques Roadshow* expert's life. You are certainly responsible for destroying the dream of an exotic holiday, and often you spark a heated family argument about who told the other it was a 'wrong 'un' all along.

In the 1970s you could have been confident, in the collectables area at least, that what you saw was what you got. Now you have to be suspicious of all subjects. Although collectors have appreciated dolls and scientific instruments, to take just two examples, for decades, the six figure prices realized at auction by collectables of all types are a phenomenon of the late 20th century. It is these prices, of course, that fire the imagination of the forgers and have led to an astonishing variety of fakes and 'honest' reproductions in the last 20 years.

The majority of the fakes in circulation were bought at markets, car-boot sales and uncatalogued auctions. The common thread running through each of these venues is that there was no indication given in writing about the date of the object in question. This leaves it to the buyer to make up his or her own mind, often with disastrous results. It is almost impossible to make a sensible judgement about an object if you are not familiar with the subject, so read up, visit museums and auctions, handle the authentic wherever possible, and when you buy ensure you get a written receipt declaring the date of the object unambiguously.

Although you should be suspicious of a collectable found at a knock-down price at a car-boot sale, don't dismiss it altogether – great discoveries are made in just such places every month. You will find vital information and tips to arm you against fakes in the following section, whether you are interested in teddy bears or golf balls, scrimshaw or a Stradivarius – happy hunting!

# AUTOMATA

Some of the most exciting finds on the *Antiques Roadshow* have been automata, which can be described as sumptuous mechanized amusements for adults. Automata were expensive luxuries even at the time they were made, and only the very wealthy were able to afford the more magnificent examples. Their golden period was between 1850 and 1914, when the craftsmen employed by Paris firms such as Roullet & Decamps, Gustave Vichy and Leopold Lambert produced examples of a magnificence and complexity that have never been surpassed. The designers of automata took their inspiration from variety entertainments and circus acts, from real life characters and situations as well as scenes drawn from imagination or satire. The results are a fascinating diversity of styles, sizes, sophistication, humour and attractiveness, with examples such as a rabbit emerging from the middle of a cabbage and a seated Arabian figure that smoked real cigarettes.

In 1980, during a *Roadshow* at Bognor Regis was the most sensational discovery of all, a figure of a bird trainer by perhaps the most highly regarded of all the Parisian makers, Gustave Vichy (*see above right*). Charles, as he was known by the owner, was an impressive automaton of great complexity and quality and in good original condition. An acknowledged rarity, in 1980 he was valued at £3,000 to £5,000. Sixteen years later Charles came to Sotheby's for auction, where he fetched a staggering £84,000.

Automata are scarce, and sums of over £100,000 have been paid at auction for large complex examples made by the desirable factories. Attracted by these prices, reproductions and outright fakes are now in circulation, so take care before committing yourself to buying what may appear to be a bargain.

One style that is currently being copied extensively is a bisque-headed doll well-dressed in

*This automaton of the Bird Trainer by the 19th-century master Gustave Vichy commanded the highest price at auction because it was complex and rare.*

*The figure, which is roughly half life-size, is dressed in its the original costume, which is in good condition.*

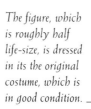

*This domestic scene of a seated Pierrot writing a letter is a modern copy of the 19th-century original made by a skilled contemporary maker, Michel Bertrand.*

*Bertrand's name is on every automaton.*

*Today these facsimiles look brand new, but it will be very difficult to differentiate between a copy and the genuine in 50 years.*

*BELOW RIGHT: Pierrot writer automaton by Michel Bertrand, late 20th century, 64 cm (25 in), £12,075*

*Automaton of a Bird Trainer by Gustave Vichy, 19th century, 102 cm (40 in) high, £84,000*

satins and silks, standing on a square velvet-covered base and moving her arms. Often such an automaton is displayed within a glazed case or beneath a glass dome with the figure standing beneath a leafy bower of fabric and dried flowers. A yellowing label bearing details of a 19th-century exhibition in France is often found stuck to the base of the figure or applied to the case. You should be suspicious if the figure and its costume are extremely dirty, particularly if it has been protected by a glazed case or a glass dome. Watch the automaton in action, it should move smoothly through a complex pattern of movements. Look carefully at the bisque head; check for cracks and see whether it is stamped with a company name or mark. Finally, listen to the tune played by the musical movement concealed inside (one fake, which was extremely convincing at first glance, was found to be playing the theme tune from *The Godfather* film).

Collectors are only willing to pay high prices for examples in good, unrestored condition with the authentic vintage costume and accessories. When buying an automaton it is important not only to check the exterior, but also to confirm that the internal mechanism and linkages are original and working. The unscrupulous have been known to construct two automata from a single example; one using the genuine mechanism but with a new body, the other using the genuine body but with a new mechanism.

*The doll looks tatty and dirty.*

*Always check the mechanism, firstly to make sure it exists and secondly to see the automaton in motion.*

THE BIRD GIRL

*A yellowing fake label, suggesting the automaton was made by Gaston Decamps, has been stuck to the base of the figure.*

*Fake automaton of the bird girl, 20th century, £100*

# BISQUE-HEADED DOLL

A few years ago a rare bisque-headed doll sold for a record-breaking £188,500. Such prices almost inevitably lead to the appearance of fakes on the market. Indeed, bisque-headed dolls are the type most frequently reproduced as they are both desirable and expensive. They are also simple to replicate as they were originally mass-produced from moulds.

Bisque (porcelain which has been tinted but left unglazed) was used for dolls' heads from the 1850s in Germany and the 1860s in France. Huge numbers of dolls were produced, particularly by the German manufacturers, and large numbers still exist today. Bisque-headed dolls are categorized according to the number of the mould from which they were made (some mould numbers are rarer and more desirable than others). Mould numbers are generally found on the back of the doll's head,

beneath the wig, and comprise a series of numbers (usually three or four digits) together with initials or the trademark of the manufacturer and the size (usually two digits).

Some of the most sought-after dolls today were produced by Kammer & Reinhardt, a company best known for its character dolls. The heads and faces of these character dolls were modelled on real children and, as a result, the expressions on the

## Facial features

Fakers find it particularly hard to replicate the faces of vintage dolls, whose eyelashes, eyebrows and mouths were painted before being returned to the kiln for the final seven hours of firing. The facial features on fakes are often painted after the final firing, which means they are likely to chip or flake. It is also very difficult to replicate the confident strokes of the original doll factory painters.

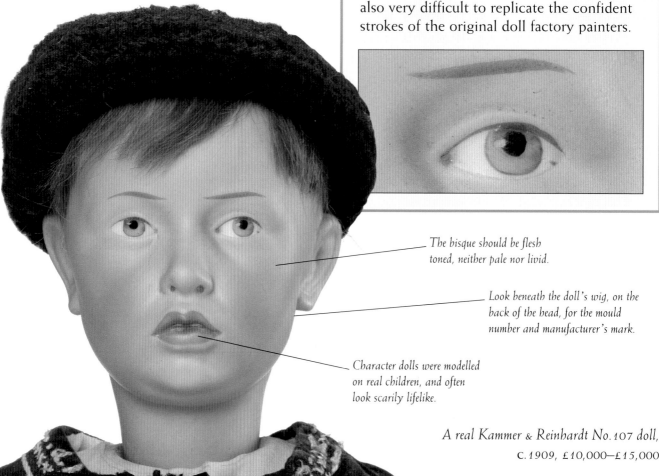

*The bisque should be flesh toned, neither pale nor livid.*

*Look beneath the doll's wig, on the back of the head, for the mould number and manufacturer's mark.*

*Character dolls were modelled on real children, and often look scarily lifelike.*

*A real Kammer & Reinhardt No. 107 doll, c. 1909, £10,000–£15,000*

faces are more realistic than the often idealized faces of other dolls. These distinctive Kammer & Reinhardt character dolls can appear wistful, sad or even cross; they were originally made in limited numbers and are particular rarities today.

While avarice is the usual motive for forgery, not all copies are made to deceive. Honest reproductions of well-known, desirable dolls from the past are made, but are identified and marked as such and usually carry in addition the name of the artist who created the contemporary copy. It is easy to be caught out if the doll is not marked at all or, more cunningly, where the mould number of the vintage doll is impressed on to the back of the head of a copy.

Side-by-side comparison with the real thing is always the best way to assess a doubtful specimen, although this is a wish not often granted. The original should, when a light is placed inside the head, appear translucent; copies can take on a blue, pink or purple hue where the porcelain is thicker than the original. The bisque of the original dolls can carry imperfections and fakers sometimes make the porcelain too smooth.

Look carefully at the body and clothes as these may offer clues about the date it was made. A contemporary body for the Kammer & Reinhardt No. 102 would be of wood and composition, jointed at the knees, hips, wrists, elbows and shoulders. It should be the correct size for the head (the two digits stamped on the back of the head usually give the size in centimetres) and show an equivalent degree of wear.

Be aware that it is still possible to buy headless bodies of the right date at fairs and at auctions.

Original clothes and accessories can add a lot to the value of a vintage doll, but modern costume can be difficult to tell from the originals. Be wary of dolls dressed in broderie anglaise or man-made fabrics; but be just as suspicious of clean-looking dolls dressed in dirty, old-looking clothes, which could be a brand new trousseau, artificially aged.

# Fake Kammer & Reinhardt No. 102 doll

*Fine lines in the bisque itself should arouse immediate suspicions.*

*The colouring of the fake is very different to that of the original.*

*The coat appears to be vintage and its use no doubt designed to alleviate any suspicions.*

*A fake Kammer & Reinhardt No. 102 doll, modern, about £100*

# STEIFF TEDDY BEAR

*There should be a hump at the top of the bear's back and the torso should be short and plump.*

*The plush should be made from mohair wool (originally from fleeces of the Turkish angora goat), and be long, straight and thickly woven.*

*The thighs should be plump, the ankles narrow, and the feet large and oval-shaped.*

*The ears should be wide apart, rounded and cupped.*

*Boot buttons (made of wood with metal loops at the back) were generally used for the eyes of early bears.*

*Early Steiff bears were made so that they could stand on all fours. They should have long curved arms, long feet and a long nose.*

The first soft bears with jointed limbs were made by Margarete Steiff in Germany in 1902. But it was an American, Morris Michtom, who devised the name 'Teddy Bear' after reputedly asking President Theodore Roosevelt's permission to use his nickname, Teddy, to describe Michtom's soft jointed bears (Roosevelt became associated with bears after refusing to shoot a cub on a hunting trip in 1902). 'Teddy's Bear' was duly produced and became an instant success; teddies became a craze with young and old and the word 'teddy bear' appeared in a dictionary for the first time in 1907, the same year as the song 'Teddy Bears' Picnic' was written. Teddies have continued to be produced in large numbers to the present day.

The boom in vintage teddy bears is a relatively recent phenomenon – the first auction to contain a large quantity of teddy bears took place in 1982. The bears in this sale were the focus of fierce competition, high prices were achieved then and prices continued to rise sharply over the following years. At a teddy auction at Sotheby's in 1989, after a heated battle between determined bidders for one vintage bear, the hammer came down at an amazing £55,000. Five years later another bear by the same German manufacturer, Steiff, reached the staggering sum of £110,000 at auction. The proud new Japanese owner even bought a separate first class seat for the return flight for his V.I.B. (Very Important Bear) so that his new addition would be comfortable on the long journey back to Tokyo!

Naturally, few of us could or would spend a six-figure sum on a teddy bear. But there are a large number of people who have become interested in vintage bears relatively recently; they may have little or no experience of handling old bears, but are willing and able to spend between £500 and £5,000 on individual examples. As with other markets that attract novice collectors, makers of fake teddy bears try to exploit potential buyers'

*Steiff Teddy Bear 1910, 43 cm (17 in) tall, £2,000*

lack of knowledge and experience. Teddy bears are a particularly attractive subject for the fakers because their raw materials are cheap and easy to obtain. So how do you tell whether you have a vintage Steiff bear or if you have been sold a pup?

Firstly, it is important to examine the bear as a whole, and not to concentrate on one or two features, such as a humped back or boot-button eyes. Most fakers get right one or two features, but never manage to encompass all the elements which make an original bear unmistakable.

Look closely at the bear's proportions. Squeeze it – if it sounds 'crunchy' and gives a little it may be stuffed with Excelsior, a material made from wood straw that was often used to stuff soft toys before 1925. The joints at the neck, shoulder and hips should be made from cardboard and should slide against one another smoothly.

The eyes on a pre-1930 Steiff bear should be deeply set and close together. Boot buttons were generally used before 1914 and glass eyes were common in the 1920s. Check for a small metal rivet or button in the left ear, which was first used as Steiff's trademark in 1904; these buttons may show an elephant (1904–5), be blank (1905–9) or be embossed with the name Steiff (1905 onwards).

The bear's coat is made from a strange cotton plush.

The eyes are of brown glass and are neither inset deeply enough nor in the right position to be genuine.

The wear and tear is in odd places, such as the top of the shoulder and all round the nose.

## Fake Steiff teddy bear

This fake bear was brought in to an *Antiques Roadshow* recently and its owners had purchased it believing it to be a vintage example. The nose is short and very sharp and the paw pads are made from leather rather than felt.

*Fake Steiff bear, late 20th century, £10*

# CAST-IRON MONEY BANKS

Over the decades these oil-based paints acquire a gentle patina, particularly in the areas of greatest use.

The cast sections of an original bank fit snugly together.

The surface should feel smooth to the touch.

The colours and details on genuine 19th-century banks were applied confidently by factory experts then heated to create a surface similar to enamel which, if damaged, will chip.

## Patents

During the 19th century, each bank design was registered at the American Patent Office. You will therefore find the patent-granted date stamped clearly on the base of a genuine American cast-iron bank. Cheap reproductions are more likely to be stamped 'Taiwan' or 'Classic Iron'. The bases of vintage banks are as well finished as the upper areas often with delicate filigree patterns allowing tantalizing glimpses of the coins inside.

Genuine Spise a Mule money bank, 19th century, £400–£600

The majority of the cast-iron toys on the market today were made in the United States between about 1870 and 1910. Many were originally produced by companies that were established manufacturers of cooking ranges, ploughs and other large cast-iron domestic and agricultural products. It did not take these companies long to realize that if they made toys, which each used a comparatively small quantity of the raw material, a highly profitable sideline could be created.

After the American Civil War (1861–65) coins were in short supply and the population was encouraged to be thrifty. One way that children were motivated to save was through the introduction of cast-iron mechanical banks which created novel and often amusing ways to part a coin from its owner.

The money banks were very popular with adults and children alike, and manufacturers vied with each other to produce banks of greater complexity and amusement potential than those of their competitors. As a result there are hundreds of different banks, which have drawn their inspiration from contemporary life and society. Circus acts and performing animals are found, others show scenes from nature or rural pursuits. Scandals, city folk and low life are all represented, as are folk tales and bible stories. There was even a bank produced which encouraged betting on the outcome of a cast-iron horse race; a mutation much more suited to the saloon than the nursery.

Although the actual process of casting iron is simple and cheap, it requires time and skill to produce a well-finished and finely cast object. The original toys are of noticeable quality, their finish is smooth and glassy to the touch, there is plenty of high and low relief detail and the various cast components fit together snugly.

Prices for banks have risen dramatically over the last 20 years and one rare design (Old Woman in the Shoe) sold at auction for over $425,000 recently. As always, these high prices have encouraged the unscrupulous. There are several different types of suspect banks in circulation today of which a new collector should be aware.

The first are the copies of genuine American banks cast in Britain and elsewhere at the same time as the originals, that is from the late 19th century until the 1930s. These are generally of good quality and often realize similar prices to the genuine American examples. The second are genuine American banks which have been either repaired or re-painted, but are passed off as being in good, original condition.

The third type is the most common; poor quality cast-iron banks looking clean, shiny and new, produced in the Far East as honest reproductions and originally sold for a few pounds each. In their newly imported condition it would be difficult to confuse these banks with vintage American examples, particularly since the bases of the modern copies are generally stamped 'Taiwan' or 'Classic Iron'.

However, these poor reproductions can be transformed into a state that is much more difficult for the amateur to detect. The identifying stamp on the base is either filled in or ground down, the banks are artificially aged by rust enhancers and are often buried or covered with a compound which gives the appearance of ingrained dirt. A general rule should be to steer clear of banks which appear rusty and very dirty.

Size is another aspect that might help the confused beginner since, as with pottery moulds, this metal casting process also involves shrinkage. Since modern reproductions are cast from the vintage American originals, the copies tend to be about an eighth of an inch smaller – very useful information if you happen to know the exact size of the original.

# FEATHERY GOLF BALLS

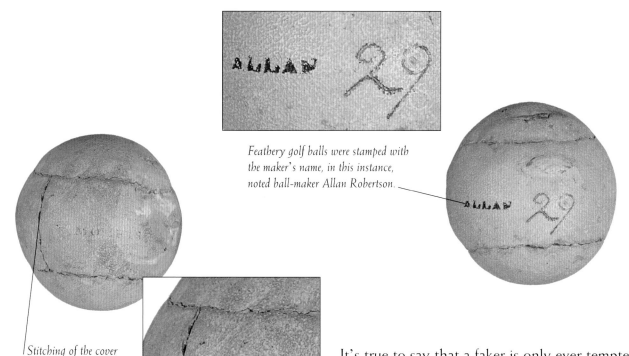

*Feathery golf balls were stamped with the maker's name, in this instance, noted ball-maker Allan Robertson.*

*Stitching of the cover was internal and invisible from the outside.*

*Feathery golf balls were not long-lasting; signs of age and play often indicate an original.*

*Three feathery golf balls made in the mid-19th century by John Sharp, Tom Morris and Allan Robertson, each showing some signs of wear and traces of original paint.*

It's true to say that a faker is only ever tempted to reproduce an original once that original has commanded sufficient value on the open market to make it worth his or her while. In this instance, the advantage is that prices of original feathery golf balls have only recently reached the dizzying heights of £5,000–£10,000 each for early balls in fine condition. Therefore the majority of replicas are all still very modern and have yet to obtain any patina of age, making them far easier to identify than many other fakes.

The feathery (or feather) golf ball was made prior to 1860 out of a leather covering stuffed with feathers. They were made by professional ball-makers, many of whom lived in Scotland. It was a skilled and painstaking art and even the most expert ball-maker was only capable of making three or four balls per day.

The feathers, plucked from a goose or chicken, were first boiled to improve their malleability. The leather cover was then stitched together leaving a small aperture and soaked in alum and water.

*Feathery golf balls by John Sharp, Tom Morris and Allan Robertson, mid-19th century, £6,000–£10,000*

# Fake feathery golf ball

Once boiled, the feathers were stuffed inside the cover, which was stitched up and left to dry. As the drying process took place the feathers expanded and the leather cover contracted, leaving a small, hard ball which, when painted white and stamped with the maker's name, was then ready for use on the golf course.

The main give-away signs of a feathery ball being a modern reproduction are the colour of the leather, looking obviously new or showing signs of having been stained to give it the appearance of age, and the lack of any wear on the leather by either handling or playing. External stitching is another good indicator.

What is often confused with the feathery golf ball is the fives ball, used in a game played with a racket or a gloved hand during the 19th century. The fives ball also has a leather cover, but it is stitched together like the segments of an orange, the seams radiating from top to bottom. The feathery ball, however, is cut from two round pieces of leather for the top and bottom, joined by a rectangular piece for the middle.

Being made from leather and hit by an iron club, the life of a feathery golf ball was not long and several balls would have been used in every round of golf. It was the introduction of rubber, or the gutta percha ball, in the middle of the 19th century that heralded the end of the feathery. These new balls were popular for their durability, and had two other advantages: they were made from inexpensive raw materials and, most importantly, they could be produced from iron moulds in considerable quantities, against which the feathery ball-makers could not compete.

The scarcity of these original feathery golf balls, in good condition and stamped by one of the great ball-makers such as William Gourlay or Tom Morris, is reflected in the considerable prices collectors are now prepared to pay.

*The leather is smooth and shiny, showing no signs of wear.*

*The dark brown pattern indicates that the leather might have been stained to imitate ageing.*

## Visible stitching

On this example of a modern reproduction feathery golf ball, the stitching is very evident on the outside of the leather and the seams feel rough to the touch. The seams of original featherys are far more delicate and indiscernible.

*Fake feathery golf ball, modern, £50–£80*

# SCRIMSHAW

*These three scrimshaw whales' teeth display characteristic designs used by 19th-century scrimshankers. Also note the yellow patina of age, which can only be achieved with period pieces. The top example displays inlaid coloured wax decoration, a feature never seen on the reproduction, or fake, scrimshaw.*

The thriving whaling industry that grew up in the 19th century was fuelled by the great international demand for whale oil, which was used for domestic heating and lighting. The whaling fleets from the east coast of North America and several British ports produced both the raw material as well as craftsmen sailors, who passed time on long voyages by working on an exquisite art form known as scrimshaw. The name refers both to the act of making a piece of decorative ware using whale products and to the completed art form.

Although the earliest recorded date for a scrimshawed whale's tooth is believed to be 1821, there can be little doubt that this craft was being practised in the late 18th century, when whaling first became an industry. The raw materials used were whales' teeth, bones and baleen, a dark-coloured material taken from the roof of the mouth of a sperm whale, as well as walrus tusks, known as 'morse' ivory. The scenes most commonly engraved on these teeth and bones were images of hunting the whale, although several also incorporated more sentimental compositions, such as portraits of loved ones and images of home life.

There are two distinct forms of bogus scrimshaw on the market, namely engraving replicating the 19th-century style, often including an old date but having being produced in the last 20 or 30 years, and the plastic resin reproduction. The first category is more difficult to identify, since in many respects they are direct copies of the original, however, a modern piece of whale ivory tends to be a much brighter white in colour than a 19th-century example, and the quality of engraving tends to be of a much higher standard. The traditional method of identifying a resin tooth is the heated needle test, genuine whale bone being

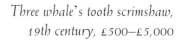

*Three whale's tooth scrimshaw, 19th century, £500–£5,000*

# Resin scrimshaw

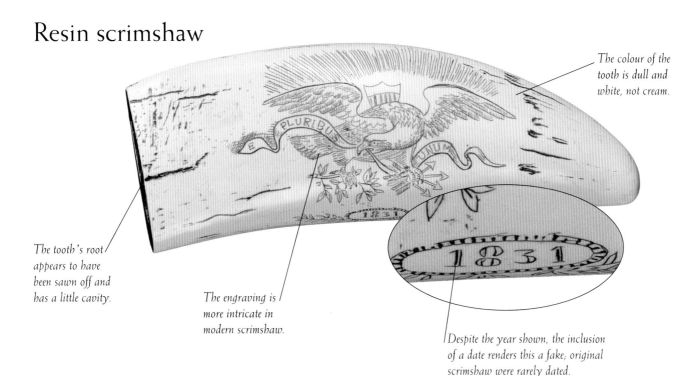

The colour of the tooth is dull and white, not cream.

The tooth's root appears to have been sawn off and has a little cavity.

The engraving is more intricate in modern scrimshaw.

Despite the year shown, the inclusion of a date renders this a fake; original scrimshaw were rarely dated.

impenetrable. However, unless one heats the needle to an almost white heat, the resin will prove difficult to melt. The more readily identifiable factors are the colour of the resin and the shape of the root.

These injection moulded resin teeth were produced in the United States during the 1960s and 1970s. The majority incorporate designs that are almost too good to be true, since they portray either famous ships or personalities, and are dated, a factor that is extremely unusual in the original. Examples of the titles of fake teeth are the *Chesapeake*, HMS *Victory*, Ship *Susan*, the *Southern Star*, *US Constitution*, and the Ship *Mercator*. Other resin wares include walrus tusks measuring either 40, 50, 60 or 70 cm (16, 19, 23 or 28 in) in length, pan bones measuring 43 by 10 cm (17 by 4 in), and ostrich eggs on stands measuring 20 cm (8 in) in height.

As with many fakes and reproductions, the first indication that pieces may be a copy is the price. If the asking price is too low, then the piece is more likely than not a fake, since good original scrimshaws rarely slip through the net.

## Root cavity

Original scrimshaw has a distinct root cavity in the base of the whale's tooth, which extends 5–8 cm (2–3 in) up into the tooth. The recent resin examples are normally cut off at the base and the cavities are much smaller.

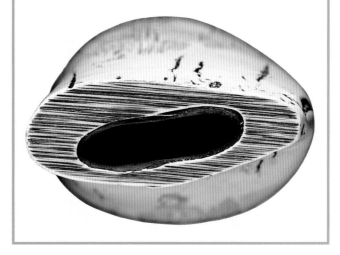

*Resin scrimshaw,*
*modern, £15–£50*

# PRISONER-OF-WAR SHIP MODELS

*The French prisoners knew all the intricacies of a working ship and they would often have seen ships in dry dock for repairs. This gave them an idea of the shape of the ship below the waterline, as seen in this correct hull shape. The detail of the bows show the finely executed decorative beakhead and carved female figurehead, together with anchor and pinned planking to the hull.*

Delicate models of naval ships were made by French prisoners-of-war when they were incarcerated in British gaols and the floating ship 'hulks' during the Napoleonic Wars of 1799–1815.

Unlike today, a prisoner in the early 19th century was not given regular food and water. Therefore, unless the inmate had a private income to buy provisions, the only two methods of survival were either to be a successful gambler or to produce wares that could be sold at the local market. Such goods included small mechanical toys, boxes decorated with coloured straws and ship models. Many of the inmates had been pressed into the navy from the French port of

*Rigging was thought to have been made from plaited human hair but in every instance the hair has deteriorated and has been replaced with twine.*

*This early 19th-century prisoner-of-war bone model displays the fine lines of a 46-gun war ship.*

*Intricate details of masts and rigging are accurate in the original models.*

*The horn strakes are clearly seen below the row of gun ports.*

*Prisoner-of-war bone model of a 46-gun war ship, early 19th century, £5,000–£25,000*

Dieppe, where there had been a long tradition of workshops producing decorative works in ivory. Therefore there was already a source of high-quality craftsmanship in the prison community who could work in bone and train other prisoners.

There are two distinctive criteria for identifying models made in the early 19th century and termed 'prisoner-of-war models' and those of a later date made by English model-makers as reproductions. The first of these is the basic construction material. The original models were normally made from beef bones left on the side of plates after the roast had been consumed. The panelling along the sides, called 'strakes', was made from animal horn. Both of these raw materials were readily available at no cost from within the confines of the prison walls. In contrast, the later models sometimes have hulls planked in ivory veneer, often made from piano keys. The original models have dark flecks in the grain of the planking and spars and they are ash-white in colour. The later ivory models have a much tighter grain with no flecking and are more creamy in colour.

The second clear method of differentiating between real and fake models is to look at the shape of the hull and the detailing of the mast, spars and rigging. The French prisoners were all experts in the art of seamanship and had full knowledge of the different parts of a ship. Therefore, original prisoner-of-war models are accurate both in design and detail. Models made by landlubbers are often crude in design, with the hull shape below the waterline being very fanciful and bearing little resemblance to a real ship.

As with so many antiques, the crucial difference between an original piece and a copy is determined by the quality, which can be discovered by any collector with experience of looking at comparable examples in public and private collections.

*Reproduction prisoner-of war ship model, 20th century, £500–£1,500*

## Deck details

Another tell-tale indication of an original model is the inclusion of details associated with life on board. These include water barrels, a ship's bell, a capstan, and netting where crews' hammocks were hung.

# Reproduction ship model

*The bone of this ship is still very white and there is no patina of age.*

*Often reproductions are easy to spot because they are factually inaccurate. The proportions of this model are very poor and it lacks in quality details.*

# MOTORING MASCOTS

In the early years in the history of the motor car, vehicle manufacturers produced a range of 'horse-less carriages' which were, in the main, bereft of any decoration. Notable exceptions were the standing figure of a blacksmith on the Vulcan in 1903 and the famous 'Spirit of Ecstasy' designed for Rolls-Royce by Charles Sykes in 1911. By about 1905 the avid motorist could purchase a mascot from accessory outlets who predominantly specialized in separate motoring horns, picnic sets and luggage, although it was not until the 1920s that the range in motoring mascots had become more extensive.

The French designer René Lalique created his first glass mascot, a dragonfly with wings folded, in 1915, and his workshop later went on to make a wide range of glass mascots including a cockerel, frog, eagle's head and mermaid. Throughout Europe and North America both the accessory suppliers and the motor manufacturers produced a huge range of mascots in bronze, chromed metal, glass and brass in every type of animal, human form and fanciful design imaginable. Unfortunately, the copying of such small-size sculptures has been prolific and it would not be an understatement to say that in all probability the majority of mascots offered for sale today are not originals and have been made within the last 20 to 30 years.

The one underlining factor to identify the original from a later copy is, as with all antiques, quality. Following this, the patina of age is also a good guideline; however this can be quite misleading, as many of these replicas are now of some considerable age themselves, and there are signs of corrosion, oxidization and general wear on many of the reproductions.

In identifying particular examples, Lalique glass mascots were originally made to be mounted on

*The bronze now has a patina of age which proves its originality.*

*The radiator cap indicates the model's purpose as a motoring mascot.*

*Bronze Bibendum mascot made by Generes et Cie for the Michelin company in France, 1922, £4,000–£5,000*

## Reproduction mascot

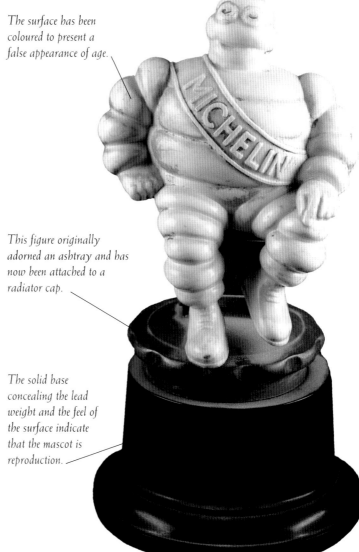

*The surface has been coloured to present a false appearance of age.*

*This figure originally adorned an ashtray and has now been attached to a radiator cap.*

*The solid base concealing the lead weight and the feel of the surface indicate that the mascot is reproduction.*

illuminated chrome bases with a collar that fitted snugly around the base; there is sometimes a significant ring mark where the metal touched the glass. The original mascots should be etched 'R. Lalique, France'. Sometimes the initial 'R' has been added later, clearly identifying it as being a more recent example tampered with to indicate an earlier date of manufacture.

Modern reproductions of the glass mascots made by Lalique and Red Ashay are currently being made in the Czech Republic; however the quality is poor and they are produced in some exotic colours not recorded by the original makers. Another common ploy by the deceiver is to irradiate a plain glass mascot giving it a colour tinge and therefore making it potentially more valuable. The colours obtainable by such methods are purple and these mascots should be treated with caution.

Sand casts are often used to make copies of metal mascots and can be quite easily identified by the method of their construction. The original mascot is impressed front and back into a bed of sand and the imprint filled with a molten metal. When cooled the two halves of the mould are welded together, with the joint between both halves filed smooth. The original mascot will have had clearly defined details on the surface, whereas the sand cast copy has only blurred outlines of details. The file scratches on the sides can also often be seen.

The buying of an original mascot may appear to have similarities to the pitfalls of buying a second-hand car, however there are many reputable dealers and auction houses who both vet and guarantee the authenticity of the products they sell. Collectors should be very wary of the market-stall-holder or car boot sale-vendor, often posing as an official dealer, who is not prepared to give a fully descriptive receipt.

*Plastic figure of Bibendum,*
*£40–£60*

### Resin reproductions

Another popular method for manufacturing fake motoring mascots is by using an injection-moulded resin sprayed with a metallic paint or actually plated with metal. They are then mounted on a weighted base to give the impression that the mascot is fully metal cast.

# BOX SEXTANTS

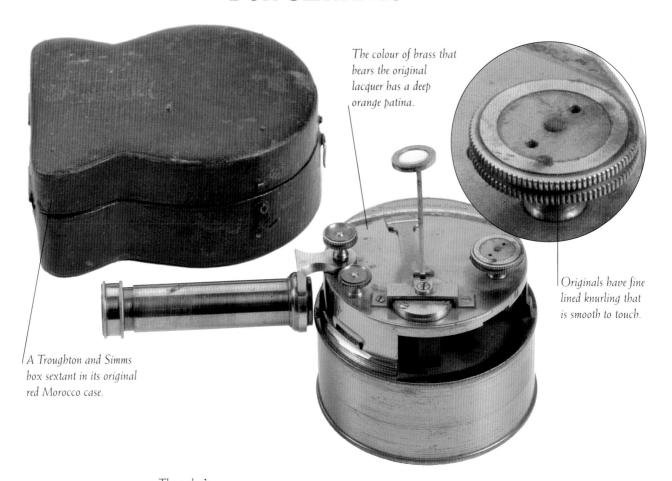

*The colour of brass that bears the original lacquer has a deep orange patina.*

*Originals have fine lined knurling that is smooth to touch.*

*A Troughton and Simms box sextant in its original red Morocco case.*

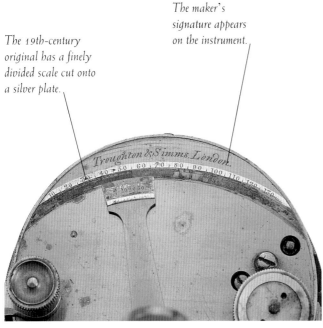

*The 19th-century original has a finely divided scale cut onto a silver plate.*

*The maker's signature appears on the instrument.*

Although fake scientific instruments have been made for at least the last 200 years, their numbers are not significant due to the fact that the skills of an optician, engraver and engineer all have to be combined to make the instrument a working tool. Such diversity had ensured that previous fakes were limited to copies of relatively simple early instruments. Notable exceptions to this rule are the pocket octagonal Butterfield dials made from silver, which flooded the market some years ago, and the 19th-century electrotype copies of astrolabes (instruments used by early astronomers to measure the altitude of stars), which it is generally assumed were made as demonstration models, the original pieces being so scarce.

*Troughton and Simms boxed sextant in original case, English, early 19th century, £300–£500*

# Reproduction sextant

This culture has radically changed since the mid-1990s. A wide variety of small-size reproduction instruments are now being manufactured in India and are available at reasonable prices throughout Europe and North America. Instruments include surveying compasses, pocket sundials, hand telescopes, theodolites, levels and marine sextants.

To identify these instruments correctly collectors should in the first instance be wary of any pieces offered in a brass-bound hardwood case or where the brass of the instrument has a bright yellow, polished colour, or a streaky light and dark colour obtained when the faker has tried to artificially age the appearance. Another sign of an instrument being bogus is if it does not actually work. Take time to use the optics and adjust the instrument and you might well identify a modern copy.

Other modern fakes include terrestrial globes made from ivory billiard balls, which are either engraved and coloured with a map of the world or, in some examples, cut in half and provided with a hinge to open out to a small horizontal sundial. Both models are mounted on ebonised wood stands. They should be avoided at all costs since almost no 18th- or 19th-century globes were made in this style.

*The scale is normally quite crude on modern examples and cut onto brass.*

*Hardwood cases are often used for reproduction sextants.*

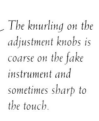

*The knurling on the adjustment knobs is coarse on the fake instrument and sometimes sharp to the touch.*

*The brass is not inlaid into the wood but is attached by small screws and lies proud of the surface.*

*Modern sextants are a much cleaner, brighter yellow.*

*Indian boxed sextant in hardwood case, modern, £15–£30*

# STRADIVARIUS VIOLINS

Name a famous violin-maker. The answer, almost every time, will be 'Stradivarius'. The fact is that Antonio Stradivari (1644–1737) of Cremona made such sonorous and good-looking instruments that he set the standard – in outline, proportions and detail – for violin-makers ever since. Tens of thousands of violins across the world carry the name 'Stradivari' or 'Stradivarius' somewhere inside. Are they fakes? If the label is a facsimile pasted into a perfectly honest instrument, perhaps in place of a previously removed label, then the intention to deceive is as clear as an agent adding a signature to an unsigned sketch or painting. It is worth double-checking the label wording, as sometimes the use of the Master's name is simply an acknowledgement of the original model. Thus, if the words '*d'après*' or '*nach*' appear before the name (meaning 'after', 'in the manner of') or any other clear qualification, there can be no serious attempt at deception. Equally '*fabriqué en France*' or '*geschützt*' (copyright) give the game away.

So well-regarded were Antonio Stradivari's violins, violas and 'cellos that their qualities of tone and workmanship were instantly recognized. Ownership of the instruments has usually been well-recorded, and today most of the violins carry the name of a celebrated owner or player.

Marie Hall (1884–1956) was one of the leading violinists of her day. She received occasional instruction from Elgar, and Vaughan Williams dedicated his *Lark Ascending* to her. She acquired the Strad that now carries her name (*see left*) in 1905. Her daughter sold it in 1968 for £22,000, a then world record price for a violin at auction.

When an expert tries to establish whether or not a violin is by Stradivari, he or she will assess the model shape and outline, the proportions, the moulding, minute detail in the f-holes, the spiral in the scroll and the purfling (strips of wood, usually inlaid, around the outside edge, front and back). Finally, they check the tone; it is widely held by professional players that Strads make a particular – the very best – sound.

In his book *How Many Strads?* (Chicago, 1945), Ernest N. Doring records all the known Antonio Stradivari instruments, including several 'whereabouts unknown'. Altogether about 600 instruments are listed; too few for a working life of 70 years. This, plus the occasional appearance of a Strad apparently not recorded in the literature, does raise the possibility of others waiting to surface. The chances of such a discovery being made at a *Roadshow* would be equal to a jackpot winner actually being in the audience during the draw of the National Lottery Live. It could be us….

*The choice, cut and colour of the wood have all been minutely copied by subsequent makers.*

*The outline, the contouring and the cutting of the 'f-holes' are all unsurpassed.*

*The most famous physical feature of a Strad is its golden varnish, the application of which is believed by some to influence the tone.*

*The 'Marie Hall' Stradivarius, 1709, over £1 million*

## Labels

Of the 20-or-so violins brought to a typical *Roadshow* (and to auction rooms all over the world) up to a quarter may bear a maker's paper label inside declaring the instrument is a Stradivarius. All labels should be treated with care, as they are easily pasted in, substituted or removed. Treat those with frayed edges with particular suspicion.

**Antonius Stradiuarius Cremonenſis Faciebat Anno 1690**

*When compared to the grain of a genuine Strad, The Rothschild (1719, above), Vuillaume's debt to Antonio Stradivari becomes clear.*

# Violin by Jean Vuillaume

High-class makers, such as the Frenchman Jean Vuillaume (1798–1875), produced Stradivarius-like instruments of exceptional quality. In the case of Vuillaume, some instruments can only be distinguished from those of the master by their labels and a varnish of glorious red tone.

It is known that Vuillaume artificially aged his own instruments by placing chamois leather on the partially dried varnish. When dry, the leather was stripped off, giving a surface that looked old.

Vuillaume's instruments are so good that questions have even been raised over the authenticity of a famous Strad, known as *Le Messie*, currently in the Ashmolean Museum, Oxford. The violin-maker is known to have made a copy of this instrument and some have questioned whether the Oxford violin – which is in immaculate condition – might not itself be a Vuillaume.

*Vuillaume's violins have a reddish varnish, rather than the golden hue associated with a Stradivarius.*

*Violin by Jean Vuillaume (1798–1875), £52,000*

# OTHER WORKS OF ART

❖◆❖

The large London or New York auction houses have 30 to 40 specialist departments. Each department may produce three to five separate sale types during the year, with several sub-groups offered within each of these. Thus it becomes clear that hundreds of different subjects make up the art market: like companies quoted on the Stock Exchange, each field has its own dynamics, its own profile of collectors at home and abroad. One day the netsuke market may rise steeply while Chinese snuff bottles remain steady and bronzes become 'volatile'. Weeks pass and a subsequent auction may show a complete reversal of trends.

In the late 20th century, as more and more people become collectors, specialist subjects have become ever more focused and greater expertise is required of expert – and forger. Today, the old-fashioned generalist, who covers as many subjects as possible, has to spread his or her extensive knowledge over a much larger area than ever before, in areas teeming with fakes and forgeries.

With a weekly *Antiques Roadshow* team of about 18 experts covering well over 100 separate subjects, we inevitably encounter objects where (out of the 10,000 to 20,000 pieces brought to a typical show) it is sometimes impossible to offer an on-the-spot opinion about value and authenticity – owing to the absence of just the right expert. In one memorable episode John Bly was examining a mystery bronze no one had been able to identify. After much puzzlement John said, 'Well I don't know what it is, but it's the best one I've ever seen!'

The following pages contain just a few examples from emerging collecting fields where fakes and forgeries have only recently started to appear. Remember, if a piece is underpriced and out of context then someone is about to make a killing – and it might not be you.

# FAR EASTERN BRONZES

Most people visiting the Far East since the end of the 19th century have brought back pieces of jade, porcelain and bronze. Taking Chinese reign marks at face value, the nine years between 1426 and 1435 were one of the most intensive bronze-producing periods in human history: almost every Chinese bronze brought to the *Antiques Roadshow* bears the four- or six-character mark of the early Ming emperor, Xuande (old-style 'Hsüan-tê'). But almost none of them are of the period. Chinese bronzes that date from a period considered to represent a climax of technological or artistic achievement bestow their 'honorary mark' on all aspiring successors, irrespective of quality. But because that essential ingredient of fakes and forgeries – namely the intent to deceive – is lacking, we should not view these potentially misleading pieces as fraudulent.

Chinese bronze technology had actually reached perfection many centuries before the Xuande period, during the legendary Shang dynasty (*circa* 1500–1000 BC) and the following Zhou (*circa* 1027–226 BC). From the later classical texts that describe the various vessel shapes, we roughly know the function of these impressive pieces: most were for wine (storage and pouring) or food (storage and warming). They often carry inscriptions suggesting ceremonial presentation. Because of this, when they surfaced in diggings in the 9th and 10th centuries AD they were regarded as auspicious, highly prized trophies from a golden (bronze) age, and the civilization that was able to produce such craftsmanship was revered. And having been so long in the earth, chemical reactions had transformed once monochrome walls into rich tones of malachite green, powder blue and reddish rusty browns, all these colours sometimes occurring on a single piece. Thus from the Song dynasty onwards copies in the archaic style began to be made.

The Chinese antiquarian Chao Xigu wrote in the 13th century:

Bronzes which have been lying in the earth for many centuries acquire a pure blue colour like that of the kingfisher. Here and there the earth has eaten into the metal, forming holes or abrasions, very like the track of a snail. If there are markings of cutting or boring, the article is a fake. Bronzes which have been lying in water for a long period, will acquire a pure green colour, lustrous like jade. A shorter period will produce the green colour but not the lustre. It is customary for people nowadays to regard light specimens as veritable antiques, ignoring that bronzes which were originally large and thick do not become thus emaciated, but lose only about one third or one half of their weight. Where a piece has been broken and where there is no sign of a bronze colour, the blue or green [patina] having penetrated to the very bones of the specimen, such a piece is antique (unlike the piece which has been immersed in water).... Placed in a kettle and boiled for a long time, the red streaks will become more apparent. Fakes which are worked up with varnish and vermilion are thus easily detected.

The passage shows that 800 years ago ancient vessels were highly prized, and so forged, but there were scholars who were able to establish right from wrong, happy to test a bronze by scientific methods such as boiling in water.

Unlike the Shang originals, many reproductions made in the Song dynasty (960–1279 AD) had inlaid gold and silver wire ornament: lines of cloud or key-fret borders, fangs, claws, eyes and other animal motifs picked out in gold and silver alloys. This archaistic tradition carried on well into the late Ming dynasty, 600 years later. At present it is

# Reproduction Buddha

not clear how to date pieces within this span. What we can say is whether a piece is of the archaic or the archaistic period. Later pieces are usually poor on detail, with sharp edges, whereas the ancient originals have rounded detail.

Advances in cast-making and patina simulation now allow very convincing reproductions. We can now take clay samples from the earthen core often still attached to the bronze and subject them to the thermoluminescence test (*see page 177*). X-rays will usually reveal uncharacteristic inner structures.

*Buddha copies are usually coarse-featured rather than serene.*

*A matt, 'weathered' green is a tell-tale sign of a reproduction.*

## Buddhistic souvenirs

The vast majority of bronzes brought back from China, Tibet, Thailand and other Buddhist regions over the last two centuries are devotional statuettes of the Buddha or *bodhisattvas*. Poor, usually recent reproductions are spotted by their colour – some have been 'bronzed' with a combination of coppery paint and dirt, which gives very patchy results.

Beneath these skins, however, is the bronze itself. Fineness of facial expression, serenity and meditation are not qualities easily copied. A genuine piece of any age should convey these qualities.

Ever since the Beatles' pursuit of oriental enlightenment, Europe has been caught up in a hippie mysticism and there's a ready market for the Krishna 'look'. Beware of the furniture trader who shrugs his shoulders and says 'I don't really know what period it is, but it didn't cost me much.' No one today runs the risk of underselling an item when expert opinion is readily available.

*Bronze figure of a* bodhisattva, *20th century,* £100–£200

# MASATSUGU NETSUKE AND OKIMONO

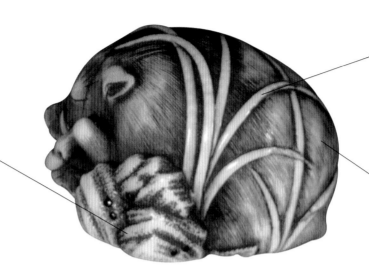

*The reeds flopping gently over the animal's back and embracing its rounded contours emphasize a state of serene slumber.*

*This is a structured rock, a craggy contrast to the floating state of its peaceful neighbour.*

*Every hair is planned, and runs parallel to its neighbour along the arched back and haunches, right down to the final folicle.*

The word netsuke, meaning 'root attach', aptly describes many of the earliest examples of this common Japanese costume accessory. The netsuke is a small carving, typically 5–10 cm (2–4 in) long, of wood or ivory, to which a cord can be tied, in order to suspend a pouch, pipe or *inro* from the wearer's belt. The majority of netsuke are drilled with two small holes (*himotoshi*) through which the cord is threaded, but, contrary to their owners' expectations, few of the small Japanese ivory carvings with such holes brought to the *Antiques Roadshow* are genuine netsuke.

From the 17th century through to the middle of the 19th century the art and craft of the netsuke-carver flourished. But in 1868, with the start of the Meiji period and after 200 years of isolationism, Japanese leaders decided to modernize, spurred on by the clear technological gap that had opened up between East and West threatening Japan's military power. A new policy of Westernization swept through all levels of life, right down to clothing. Western tailoring replaced the centuries old, elegant but pocketless kimono. Consequently an equal revolution occurred in all those traditional crafts associated with the kimono.

Defunct pouches, toggles and boxes were thrown out in their millions and craftsmen who wanted to survive turned their skills to the creation of new commodities. Instead of the anticipated decline, the traditional arts and crafts of Meiji Japan saw a remarkable renaissance, boosted by the creation of new wealth and a need for luxury goods, both at home and for the newly opened markets abroad. Craftsmanship reached new levels that have never been bettered. Meanwhile, in Europe, the old goods began to arrive by the barrel: *inro, ojime* and netsuke could be bought for a few shillings.

Years later, in contrast to the once traditional Japanese reluctance to buy second-hand goods, netsuke began to rise in value. Collecting has become expensive, and today the art of netsuke-carvers is recognized as fine sculpture in miniature, and the top names regularly exceed the £100,000 mark. One artist whose works are highly sought after is Kaigyokusai Masatsugu (1813–92) netsuke- and *okimono*-carver of Osaka. Renowned for his realism, it is said that, when a group of children failed to recognize one of the artist's carvings of mushrooms, Masatsugu destroyed the work and began afresh.

*Okimono of sleeping boar by Kaigyokusai Masatsugu, c. 1860–90, £10,000–£20,000*

This perfectionism is reflected in one of Masatsugu's favourite subjects, a boar sleeping by a rock. At just under 5 cm (2 in) the piece on the left is of netsuke proportions, but the carving has a flat bottom, which means that it was designed for sitting on a flat surface – a stand or a table – and not for 'floating' at the top of a belt or sash. So it's an *okimono* ('lucky charm'), in the netsuke tradition.

Both pieces illustrated are signed 'Kaigyokusai Masatsugu', but one is a forgery. The difference in size is not diagnostic: Masatsugu was a netsuke-carver who turned successfully to *okimono*. But there is a noticeable difference in the treatment of the reeds sprouting from the rocks. In the larger example below the reeds are well-observed and detailed, and one breaks naturalistically over the other. In the smaller carving the reeds are slimmer and less vigorous. But comparing the rocks, in the smaller example there is greater attention to texture with a contrast between the sleeping pig and its craggy rest. Herein lies the difference: deep in a dream and wrapped in reeds, one can almost see the breathing of the smaller boar. But in the larger carving the reeds distract from stillness. By giving the detail equal weight to the subject, there is no tension between elements.

Both boars are works of art. In a land where a master bestows his name and title to the worthiest successor, notions of authorship and authenticity are not as tight as those of the West. In the case of the larger piece we cannot say who is responsible, but we can say that artistically it is simply not as good. On this basis it becomes a copy.

## Masatsugu copy

*The hairs are finely lined, but not with the same care and skill, nor with a sense of flow.*

*The reeds are a separate tour de force and the rock is just a lump.*

*A signature may be that of the master or of his student, or of a person wholly unconnected with the studio.*

*Okimino of a sleeping boar, in the style of Kaigyokusai Masatsugu, late 19th century/early 20th century* £1,000–£2,000

# SNUFF BOTTLES

In Europe snuff was carried in boxes, but in China snuff came in bottles. In the late 16th and early 17th centuries Spanish merchants trading to China via the Philippines introduced powdered tobacco to the northern regions of China. By the end of the 17th century the newly established Manchu rulers of the Qing dynasty had brought the snuff habit down to the Imperial capital in Beijing, and from the early 18th century, as the custom became generally fashionable, more and more attention was given to the making of the little bottles that carried the brown powder. The Imperial workshops in Beijing began to produce bottles out of a wide variety of materials, including porcelain, bamboo, agate, jade, the bill of the hornbill bird, ivory, enamels (on copper as well as *champlevé* and *cloisonné*) and, most abundantly of all, in plain or multi-layered glass.

By the end of the 18th century any mandarin worth his snuff owned an assortment of bottles to flaunt his good taste and the depth of his pocket. Snuff bottles had become an art form, a 'collectable' fashion accessory remaining popular right through to the end of the Qing dynasty in 1912. Several years later, when an increasing number of Westerners began to realize just how fine some of these 5-cm (2-in) masterpieces were, prices for old bottles began to compete with that other oriental art form, the netsuke (*see page 162*).

Today, some of the highest prices (tens of thousands of pounds) are paid for the very top quality interior-painted snuff bottles, made of glass (sometimes coloured, but this obscures the painting) or, rarely, of hollowed rock crystal. Like the ship in a bottle, the painter's challenge is to overcome the seemingly impossible: firstly, the small size of the bottle makes it extremely difficult to manoeuvre a brush with any accuracy; secondly, as the painting is seen from the other side of the glass surface, everything has to be painted in reverse order to a normally painted image on paper. With a portrait rather than a landscape or a calligraphic text, the challenge becomes even greater.

Portrait bottles were first produced towards the end of the 19th century. The portraits were usually copied from a photograph, so it is easy to mistake a snuff bottle portrait for a photograph or transfer print. (Such techniques have been used,

*Ma Shao-Xuan was particularly famous for the quality of his calligraphy.*

*Most inside-painted snuff bottles were never used to keep snuff, for fear of damaging the painting.*

*The features of the portrait are slightly softer and a little less stiff than those on the copy.*

*The form of the bottle, with its slender shoulders, is very elegant.*

FAR LEFT: *Snuff bottle by Ma Shao-Xuan, 1907*
LEFT: *Snuff bottle by Ye Zhongsan the Elder, 1908*

# Fake snuff bottles

but the results have hitherto been crude and easily spotted.) As with the decoration of all interior bottles, a fine brush is mounted at right angles on to a fine bamboo shaft which is inserted through the neck. The artist paints by looking at the bottle face-on, while controlling the angled brush by pushing it gently towards him. He might start with the details of the face – eyes, nose and mouth – finishing with the shading and the clothes. On the finest examples, by artists such as Ding Erzhong or Ma Shao-Xuan, the reverse may be a landscape or a text dedicated to the subject, in masterly calligraphy, signed and dated.

To illustrate how widespread collecting has become, a top snuff bottle dealer recently bought a 200-year-old jade bottle with a very distinctive banding in San Francisco; some time later he found its companion bottle, carved from the very same jade boulder, thousands of miles away in Hong Kong.

Chinese snuff bottles are highly collectable because of their beauty, variety and size. With prices soaring and the nurturing of old painting skills after the political and artistic turmoil of China during much of the 20th century, market conditions are ripe for the production of high-quality fakes such as the one seen here.

*The modern artist has dusted the interiors of both these bottles with snuff, in a somewhat uniform and unnatural fashion, to make them look older.*

*These two bottle are flatter, with broader shoulders, than the originals. Also, they are identical.*

*The portrait itself has been superbly copied and there is very little difference in quality between it and the genuine example.*

## Calligraphy

The original calligraphy is beautifully written with flowing characters having both thick and thin strokes, a sign of a fine calligrapher, whereas on the modern bottle (right) the characters are written in black ink with uniformly thick strokes.

*RIGHT: Fake snuff bottle, 1980*

# BILLIES AND CHARLIES

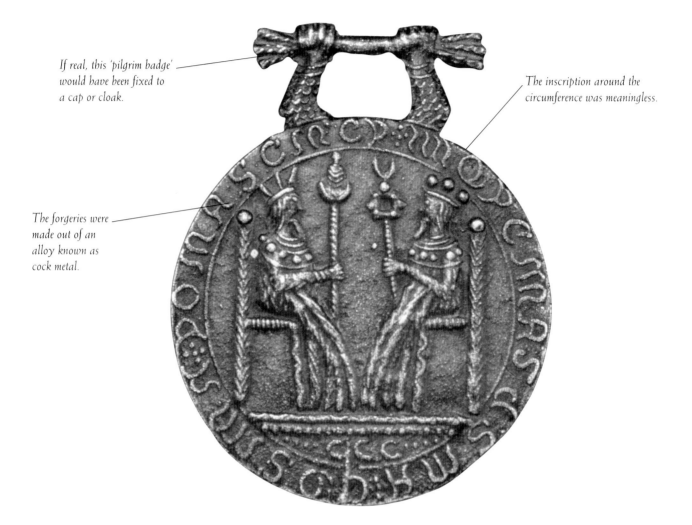

*If real, this 'pilgrim badge' would have been fixed to a cap or cloak.*

*The inscription around the circumference was meaningless.*

*The forgeries were made out of an alloy known as cock metal.*

If you had been walking through the East End of London during the mid-19th century, you may well have seen the shadowy figures of William Smith and Charles Eaton, plodding through the mud at Shadwell dock. This pair scratched a living from the relics unearthed by each day's receding tides. In 1857 business improved for Smith and Eaton (known to their friends as Billy and Charlie) as they began to hit upon all sorts of interesting finds from the 10th to the 14th centuries: small jugs, reliquaries, badges (several actually dated), and general medieval knick-knackery.

But some experts were sceptical. When the antiquarian through whom these 'Billies and Charlies' were being sold was accused of handling forgeries, a well-known scholar, Charles Roach Smith, gave evidence in court. Smith stated that these remarkable finds could not possibly be forgeries as no one could possibly have invented such an unexpected group of objects; they would need to have been fabricated out of thin air. Though the business was dented by the case, more pieces came to light and the market for these remarkable pieces recovered. In 1861 Roach Smith

*Billie and Charlie,*
*c.1860, £200–£400*

adjusted his earlier endorsement of the finds, claiming they were likely to have been produced during the reign of Queen Mary (1553–58), and were possibly replacements for devotional items destroyed during the Reformation. The debate now rekindled, and the Society of Antiquaries put on an exhibition of moulds seized (under dubious circumstances) from Smith and Eaton. They proved conclusively that these objects were being manufactured out of a copper-lead alloy known as cock metal. Despite the definitive exposé, for Billy and Charlie it was business as usual. Many more pieces were made over the next 10 years.

In fact, so many Billies and Charlies were made in little more than a dozen years (Charles Eaton died in 1870) that many collectors, embarrassed by their trophies, threw them out; it is noticeable today how many Billies and Charlies surface in people's gardens. As a *cause célèbre* they are now collectable in their own right, trading even on the Internet, reminders of how enthusiasm can lead wisdom by the nose.

If the eclectic Victorians seem gullible they can be excused. Their time was moving so fast that they simply did not know where they were. Their Empire was expanding at an unprecedented rate, and they were like children in Time's Sweetshop, not knowing which drawer to open next and hardly having time to worry about authenticity.

Occasionally Billies and Charlies are dated, which is where more deception occurs. Pieces dating to an 11th-century pre-Conquest period had hitherto all been dated in Roman numerals, but this new group were dated in modern Arabic style. This made scholars uneasy, while for Roach Smith this added to credibility since, he claimed, a forger would surely stick to known forms and conventions. This is something of a moral for the forger: don't be afraid of making something that is totally unexpected and off-the-beam.

## Victorian revivals

The Victorian Age was not one, but several ages. It was the Age of Revivals. At the start of her reign, Queen Victoria's England was immersed in a delayed spasm of the mid-18th century, the neo-Rococo – frilly Rockingham tea services with elaborate scroll handles flopping this way and that, potpourri vases smothered in encrusted flowers, deep button-backed sofas and chairs on squat cabriole legs.

A decade later comes Augustus Pugin and his followers, whisking us back into the sombre medieval period, passing under Gothic arches, ecclesiastical ornament gracing every nook and cranny, funereal dark oak furniture, charged with escutcheons and trophies of chivalry.

At the same time, Sir Walter Scott took his readers on crusades with the Knights Templar, while in Germany Richard Wagner joined Tristan, Parsifal and other Knights of the Round Table all singing along with the burghers of Nuremburg. 'Mad' King Ludwig of Bavaria hallucinated in a Disney-esque land of pinnacles and turreted fairytale castles and the pre-Raphaelite Brotherhood escaped to the blue Tuscan hills of Dante's early Italian Renaissance.

A brief sobering up followed with a Classical Revival, ensued by another escape, this time into the 1,001 Nights of the Orient. In 1859 Edward Fitzgerald published his translation of *The Rubáiyát of Omar Khayyám*, while whole Chinese and Japanese symphonies and serenades were painted in this or that colour by impish James MacNeill Whistler, conjuring Kyoto quaysides from the muddy banks of the Thames.

# GALLÉ CAMEO GLASS VASE

*There is only a narrow collar of overlay.*

*The signature on this piece is on the neck at the back. Signatures on genuine pieces are invariable on the side which is sparse in decoration. The mistake the fakers often make is to make the signature too obvious.*

*The decoration is distributed evenly and there is a large area of space to balance it.*

*There is a narrow foot rim of overlay and the foot is slightly flared.*

French art glass, particularly the cameo, has been popular with collectors almost continually since the 1960s, with market activity peaking in the late 1980s. With this pronounced interest came the inevitable copies. In the early stages many of the cameo pieces seen with 'Gallé' signatures started their existence as unsigned modern glass made with no intention to deceive, but subsequently were signed by unscrupulous traders. This was often achieved by acid etching away an area of existing relief decoration to establish a signature in relief. A new collector should not refer to marks alone when buying a piece of cameo glass; if possible he or she should seek professional help.

In recent years many copies have been seen in antique fairs and markets, all made in the same manner as Gallé would have produced his and bearing his facsimile signature. They are sold as 'Gallé-style', which is correct but open to abuse by the fact that they bear his signature. Fortunately, the pieces brought to the *Antiques Roadshow* for appraisal are in the main genuine, having been in the owner's family for many years or have been possibly bought unexpectedly in a job lot some considerable time ago, and their true value only recently recognised. Pieces that have been recently bought cheaply and with little experience generally turn out to be disappointments.

## Cameo glass

To produce cameos the glass is blown, then immersed whilst hot into glass of a different colour that will pleasingly contrast with the colour of the vessel. A decorative design is then either carved with a wheel or etched with hydrofluoric acid into the glass 'overlay' to reveal the ground colour beneath.

*Genuine Gallé cameo glass vase,*
*c.1905, £8,000*

# Fake Gallé vase

The technical procedure to produce a genuine Gallé vase and that to produce a fake is largely the same, so it is not always obvious that a piece is not genuine. Detection has become increasingly difficult in recent years as the quality of the fakes has increased tremendously.

Sometimes a collector can be puzzled by a name on a piece that is not familiar to him or her. It could be a genuinely old piece from a little-known factory and not a modern copy of Art Nouveau cameo glass. Recently, an authentic Art Nouveau glass vase came to light, beautifully carved with floral motifs and made in the Russian Imperial workshops. The original Russian marks for Nicholas II had been removed, however, and a 'Gallé' signature put in their place. In this instance the piece was not a fake Gallé glass, only the signature was false – added because at the time of the deception, Gallé was far more commercial than Russian glass.

The genuine Gallé vase (left) is of a type called 'mould-blown' or 'blow out'. As the name suggests, it is made by blowing the glass into a pre-formed shape that gives a more substantial and 'rounded' look to the decoration. The colours used to decorate the two pieces are similar, but the form the decoration takes is less naturalistic on the fake (right) in comparison to the original.

On the inside of the fake, the amber colour where the swelling for the fruit is, has been removed by what appears to be grinding, whereas on the original the removal of colour is much more subtle as if it has been 'wiped away'. The weight of the fake vase, whilst being smaller than the genuine piece, is uncharacteristically heavy.

There are numerous regular auctions of genuine French cameo glass, where a budding collector can view and handle pieces and over a period of time train the eye. Seek out specialist dealers who will be happy to advise a new would-be client.

*The whole of the neck is covered with overlay.*

*The decoration has been spread over a large area attempting to maximise the effect.*

*The fruit on this piece, whilst standing out in plump relief, is not as 'lush' as on the original.*

*The signature here is a very good likeness but not quite right and its orientation is wrong. The signature on the genuine piece is on the neck.*

*The foot is rounded instead of flared.*

*Fake 'Gallé' cameo glass vase, c.1990, £80*

# BRONZE AND IVORY FIGURE

Figures fashioned from ivory combined with another contrasting material, such as a precious metal, bronze, marble, hardstone or wood, are referred to as Chryselephantine. The technique of ivory carving goes back to the earliest days of humankind and was practised continuously up to the late 20th century, when a ban on the sale of new ivory and ivory goods was introduced.

At the end of the 19th century an enormous amount of ivory was being fashioned into knife handles, billiard balls, piano keys, inlays for decorative furniture and a myriad of other 'useful' items. A large proportion of this ivory came from the Belgian Congo. Indeed, the surplus of ivory in Europe was so great at this time that the Belgian government called on the country's artists to use it as the basis for their works of art, providing further encouragement through commissions and exhibitions. Symbolist and Art Nouveau artists, who wished to distance themselves from the 'established' art movement, delighted in using ivory as a new means of expression.

Ferdinand Preiss (1882–1943), a German, was one of the finest ivory carvers of his generation. He was apprenticed to Philipp Willmann, then worked for a time in Baden-Baden for the firm of Haebler, before leaving with a colleague, Arthur Kassler, to form Preiss & Kassler – turners and carvers in ivory – in Berlin. The company's earliest compositional figures were classically

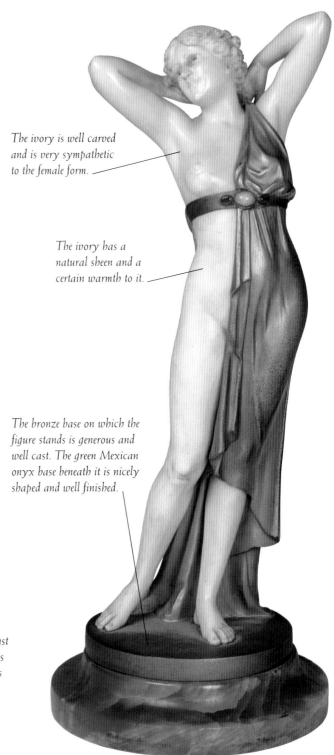

*The ivory is well carved and is very sympathetic to the female form.*

*The ivory has a natural sheen and a certain warmth to it.*

*The bronze base on which the figure stands is generous and well cast. The green Mexican onyx base beneath it is nicely shaped and well finished.*

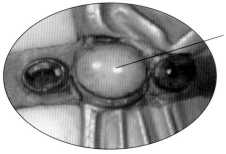

*The bronze is crisply cast and the folds in the robes look realistic. The jewels on the belt are a central opal cabochon flanked by two garnets.*

*Genuine bronze and ivory figure of Aphrodite, signed 'F. Preiss', c. 1925, £2,400*

# Fake composition figure

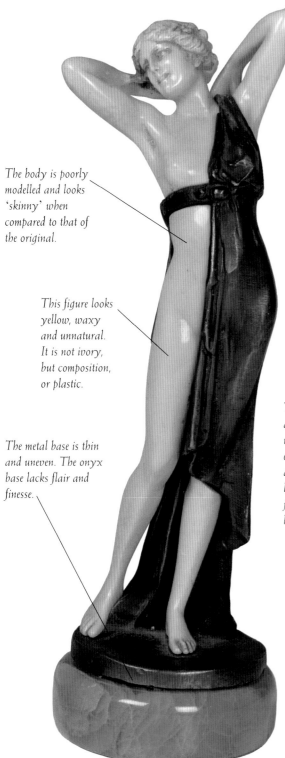

*The body is poorly modelled and looks 'skinny' when compared to that of the original.*

*This figure looks yellow, waxy and unnatural. It is not ivory, but composition, or plastic.*

*The metal base is thin and uneven. The onyx base lacks flair and finesse.*

inspired, and included one of Aphrodite, the Greek goddess of sensual love.

When trying to decide whether a bronze and ivory figure is genuine or reproduction you will need to look at the quality of the carving and detailing. Preiss's figures are very naturalistic; it should be easy to imagine the lines and curves beneath the flowing robes. A fake is unlikely to show the same attention to detail. Also, the figure should look 'right' for its age. For example, the figure on the right is skinnier and has greater muscle definition than that on the left, both sought after qualities in the late 20th century.

The signature 'F. Preiss' will either be found on the bronze base or scratched into the stone base. Often there is no signature on a fake, but if it has been produced from a mould made from a genuine piece, then the signature may then appear with poor legibility due to the poor casting.

*The metal is low-grade bronze or brass, and lacks any sense of finish. Any extra work incurred in producing these figures eats into the profits, so major short-cuts are taken, which lead to the resultant loss of quality. There are no actual jewels on this piece, although some have been implied.*

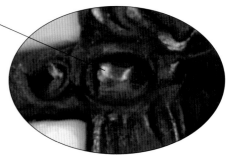

## Yellowing

Ivory does become yellow if it is kept in adverse conditions, but the discoloration is usually localized. Overall yellowing on a genuine piece may occur if it has been in a heavy smoker's room for many years. In this case, a thick layer of foul-smelling tar will need to be carefully removed.

*Fake bronze and composition figure of Aphrodite, c. 1990, about £100*

# CHRISTOPHER DRESSER VASE

Christopher Dresser (1834–1904) was a forward-looking designer who, unlike his contemporary William Morris (1834–96), embraced the machine and designed with mechanical production in mind, becoming what could be correctly described as an 'industrial designer'. Unlike Morris, who was and is a household name, Dresser remains comparitively little known, his remarkable achievements barely recognized until recent years.

Dresser's aim was to bring into every household articles that were well designed, functional, well made and affordable. A review by Dresser in the *Furniture Gazette* on 20 May 1876 stated '…it is by bringing to the homes of the people objects of art and beauty at a low price that more good is done in refining the middle and lower classes than by all the museums in existence; the effect of the latter is transitory…'

A botanist by training, Dresser had a strong understanding of many materials, especially metals and glass, but also ceramics. He worked over a long period with various potteries, beginning, it would seem, with Minton prior to the London International Exhibition of 1862. Many of his designs were for pieces that emulated Chinese *cloisonné* enamels, with their vivid turquoise backgrounds. He also created some extraordinary designs for Wedgwood that tended towards organic highly formalized plant forms.

Dresser's work with the Linthorpe Pottery in North Yorkshire, the first manufacturer to produce Art Pottery by mass-production methods, was very fruitful. His pieces from the 1870s and 1880s may well have been influenced by examples of Peruvian pottery seen in the Sir John Soane Museum in London, and he was probably also

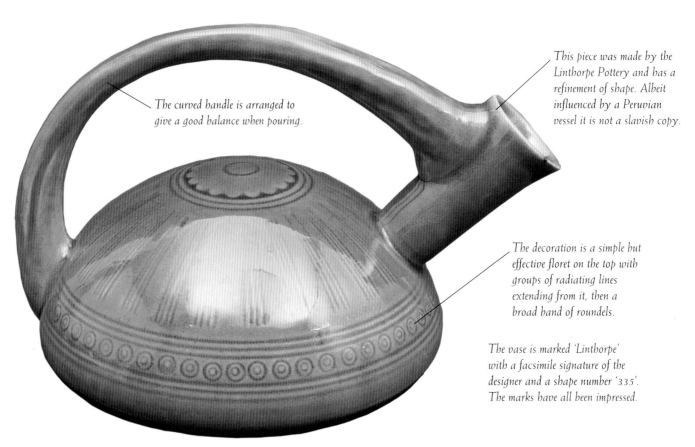

The curved handle is arranged to give a good balance when pouring.

This piece was made by the Linthorpe Pottery and has a refinement of shape. Albeit influenced by a Peruvian vessel it is not a slavish copy.

The decoration is a simple but effective floret on the top with groups of radiating lines extending from it, then a broad band of roundels.

The vase is marked 'Linthorpe' with a facsimile signature of the designer and a shape number '335'. The marks have all been impressed.

*Genuine Christopher Dresser (Linthorpe) vase, 1880, £2,250*

# Fake Christopher Dresser vase

*This vase was also influenced by Peruvian pottery, but has nothing to do with Dresser. It was most probably made in Belgium.*

*The glaze is very similar to the streaky glazes seen on Linthorpe and Ault pieces, but would not convince the trained eye. This particular blue would be unusual on a Linthorpe vase.*

*The vase has a very similar body shape to a Linthorpe vase that has two spouts and is decorated with a stylized face. A similar Ault model also exists with two spouts, one narrow and one flared, both linked to a curved handle.*

aware of *Perou et Bolivie* (1880) by the French archaeologist Charles Wiener, which included illustrations of pieces with incised decoration.

By 1882, the pottery's success was faltering and Dresser decided to leave along with Henry Tooth, who had produced the daring glaze effects on many of Dresser's pots. The break-up sale of Linthorpe took place in 1890, when William Ault bought many of the factory's moulds. Three years later Dresser signed a contract with Ault to provide him with designs to the exclusion of any other potters.

## Dresser marks

The mark on the bottom of this piece shows an Ault Pottery mark and a Dresser facsimile signature. The Ault mark if correct would be in relief, unlike this mark, and the signature would not be rubber stamped. When the signature is this small, it is normally found on Linthorpe pieces and is impressed. When it appears on Ault pieces it appears alone, without the Ault mark, and in a much larger size. The two marks never appear together, so these marks must be fake, although the vase does date from the late 19th century.

*Fake Christopher Dresser vase, possibly* c. *1890, £100*

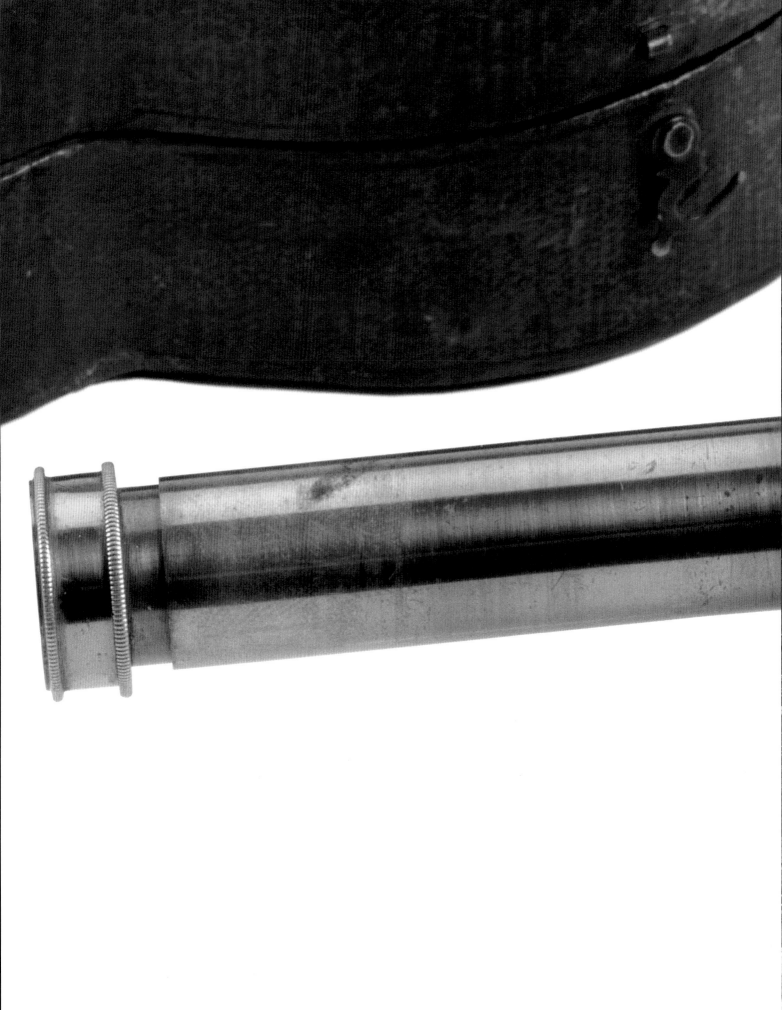

# SCIENTIFIC INVESTIGATIONS

We have come a long way from the 13th century scientific techniques of Chao Xigu – happy to date a bronze by boiling it in water (*see page 160*). A number of investigative techniques are available today, providing sometimes valuable clues about a piece that cannot be furnished by the naked eye. Nevertheless, the results of scientific analysis should usually be calibrated against works with known dates. This does not mean that the boffins have been idle. Far from it: Chinese scientists have used cadmium to induce fluorescent X-rays from pieces of Straits Chinese porcelain and bombarded specimens with low energy gamma rays to distinguish between gold plating and wrapping. Scientists in London have detected fake 9-carat sovereigns by the analysis of induced electric pulses, and the carbon dating of the eventually fake Turin Shroud is well known. Such techniques are generally expensive and, therefore, reserved for ancient artefacts where no other evidence is available. Collectors of fine art and antiques are justifiably reluctant to allow scientists to drill or chip the requisite sample from their newly acquired treasure.

## Chemical/metallurgical analysis

This form of analysis has been around for a long time. The analysis may be relatively straight forward, depending on the complexity of the material and the required accuracy of the results. Many methods are available: from school chemistry standard right up to expensive laser mass spectroscopy, for example, where exact chemical compositions can be determined. Post World War II fakes of pewter items can be tested for a characteristically high lead content. Brass items can be attributed to later than 1770 if the zinc content is higher than 30 per cent, when the use of mineral zinc became widespread. In fact any material can be tested to discover whether it contains substances that should or should not be present.

## Computer recognition and databases

The age of the personal computer and the Internet allow for the storing and cataloguing of many works of art. Computers can now be trained to recognize the attributes of a large number of objects, such as marks. This wealth of information often allows a much swifter identification of an item, often without the need of an expert.

# Conventional optical methods

There are many instances where the human eye is just not powerful enough to make out all the clues that might contribute to the history of a work of art. Engraved decoration on silver items may often have been sharpened up and, if used well, a powerful optical microscope may allow the detection of the lines of an engraving tool. Careful examination of the hallmark of a silver item may reveal signs that the hallmark has been taken from another piece and soldered on to falsify its origins.

# Radiocarbon dating (C14)

All living things are composed principally of carbon, of which a small quantity is the radioactive carbon isotope carbon-14. Whilst alive, the proportion of carbon-14 in the organism is equivalent to the concentration found in the atmosphere of the day. Once dead, this proportion is fixed and the carbon-14, being radioactive, starts to decay slowly away. By measuring the activity of a sample, the date of death of the material can be established. However, this is definitely not an everyday method for an antiques collector. It is very expensive and can only be carried out on once-living material, such as wood, bone or fabric. After adjustments and calibrations have been made (using tree-ring and other forms of absolute dating) accuracy can be established typically to within 2–10 per cent. Dates can be obtained for samples up to 100,000 years old, and had the technique been available at the time the 'Piltdown Man' would instantly have been exposed.

# Thermoluminescence: (TL testing)

This technique is used for dating ceramics. During the life of a piece, ionizing radiation, mainly from the sun, frees electrons to move through the crystal lattice of the ceramic object's microscopic structure, until trapped by tiny imperfections. This process continues until the material is heated where the trapped electrons are released producing light. The longer the piece is exposed to radiation without heating, the more intense is its accumulated luminescence.

For a piece of ceramic the luminescence 'stop-watch' is set at the last firing. The intensity of subsequently accrued luminescence can be measured by drilling a very small sample of clay (no bigger than a pencil tip) and subjecting it to heat under laboratory conditions. By measuring the released luminescence its age since last fired can be calculated. The method is reasonably accurate if properly calibrated and particularly useful for collectors of earlier periods such as Han and Tang dynasty funerary figures.

# Ultraviolet light

Ultraviolet lamps are becoming an increasingly common tool in uncovering forgeries and fakes. Different materials react in different ways to illumination by ultraviolet light. Discontinuities in stone of a light hue, such as limestone, marble or alabaster, show up well, illustrating any past repairs in the sculpture or whether it has been made up from old fragments. Glass, too can be examined in this way. There are a large number of copies of 18th-century glasswork circulating today. This group of copies give collectors and dealers the most trouble, since many of their characteristics proclaim the same origins as an original. Being numerous these fakes were very common 40 years ago, and although there were several pointers available to the experienced dealer, they tended to circulate freely. Today, ultraviolet illumination provides a quick and reliable check.

The genuine article will be made of lead glass and will take on a blue hue tinged with purple. The strong yellowish-green reflection of the soda glass copies allow them to be immediately uncovered.

# X-rays

The many recent advances in the field of X-ray imaging, both for the medical and the industrial markets, have provided technology that is increasingly suitable for examining works of art. The most obvious technique is to make an X-ray image of a piece in much the same way as one would X-ray a human being. Not being made of flesh and blood, the intensity of the radiation required will be different, but the X-ray image will usually be able to distinguish objects such as supporting ironwork in sculpture.

The art world has, in recent years, taken full advantage of X-ray technology to make radiographs of the individual layers making up oil paintings. This allows experts to see all the steps in the creation of the work and not just the end, and perhaps forged, result.

# A Note on Prices in this Book

Valuing works of art is a bit like valuing shares: prices may go up as well as down. Most figures given in this book reflect an average auction-room price at the time of going to press.

Typically, about 10 per cent of works of art offered at auction fetch prices below the auctioneer's estimate, the vast majority of hammer prices fall within the (very wide) pre-auction estimates published in the catalogue, and a small but noteworthy number of works (usually at the very top end of the quality/rarity range) fetch above-estimate prices, landing them in the following day's news. The BBC's *Antiques Roadshow* generally offers auction estimates. Prices suggested in this book are offered on this basis or, occasionally, on an actual price fetched in the market place.

# GLOSSARY

**Art Deco** – name of a 1930s style of geometry, circles, arcs and rectangles first emerging in the 1920s and replacing the organic forms of the Art Nouveau: name coined from the 1925 Paris Exposition des Arts Décoratifs.

**Art Nouveau** – style of the late 19th/early 20th century particularly represented by French, Belgian and Austro-Hungarian artists: organic forms, voluptuous curves and whiplash motifs, swooning asymmetry, narcotic poppies, sex and opium.

**ball foot** – furniture foot in the form of a sphere, sometimes gripped by a claw ('claw and ball').

**baluster** – architectural term for the individual uprights supporting the handrail on a stair or balcony (ie the balustrade), each usually turned or carved with an in-and-out curved profile: from which used  to describe the same shape in ceramics, glass and metalwork, often when denoting the stem or overall form of a vessel.

**Baroque** – 17th-century decorative style epitomized by symmetric scroll-edged cartouches and panels.

**bisque or biscuit** – French term for porcelain fired without a glaze. If left *in the biscuit*, when stained with colour and fired, porcelain lends itself to the dry natural flesh tones of dolls' heads and limbs. Bisque dolls were made from the mid-19th century to the 1930s and revived from the 1960s.

**blank** – a ceramic object, usually porcelain, which has yet to be decorated, whether in the factory or outside (see *in-the-white*); of metal, a piece intended for striking with a design (eg a coin).

**blue-and-white** – term to describe (white) porcelain painted in *underglaze* blue; by extension also describes any ceramic body (especially *delftware*) painted in this style.

**bone china** – a porcelain body-recipe comprising up to 50 per cent of the traditional hard-paste formula (ie china clay and china stone) the remaining 50 per cent being calcified bones: an English invention ascribed to Josiah Spode *c*.1794 and adopted almost universally by English porcelain manufacturers from the early 19th century onwards.

**Britannia standard** – a particularly high standard of silver purity (95.8 per cent), in England compulsory for makers of plate until 1720 (thereafter optional) since when Sterling standard (92.5 per cent) is minimum British requirement for silver wares.

**burnish** – the action of buffing or polishing up a usually gold or gilded surface, whether on metalwork, gold-leafed furniture or ceramics (when an agate or beryl stone is often used).

**cabriole** – furniture term given to a goat-like, S-shaped leg tapering from a bulbous upper half to a slender lower half (from French 'to caper', goat-like). Shape especially associated with *Rococo* designs.

**carat** – 1. unit of weight for a gemstone or pearl (=200mg); 2. measure of gold purity (against maximum purity of 24 carats).

**cartouche** – panel or tablet based on a paper scroll (ie with frayed or curly edges), by extension any framed or bordered panel used as a decorative device in silver, furniture or ceramics.

**caster** – any vessel with perforated lid for dispensing powered foodstuffs or flavourings.

**celadon** – general European ceramic term for any monochrome green glaze: mainly associated with Chinese glazes of the Song and Ming dynasties. The name may be coined from a corruption of Saladin (a notable collector) or from 'Celadon', a character from French 17th-century drama, dressed in a coat of green.

**champlevé** – see *enamel*

**chasing** – reworking or re-fashioning (rather than removal by chisel) of metalwork (usually of silver/bronze).

**chinoiserie / japonaiserie** – European fantasies of Far Eastern life, peoples and landscapes, as depicted in all the decorative arts, from the mid-17th century, in the Regency period and again in the 1860s when the Aesthetic Movement sought inspiration in Japanese designs.

**chromolithograph** – a multi-coloured print produced lithographically (ie printed off several stone surfaces).

**cloisonné** – see *enamel*.

**craquelure** – a network or mesh of fine cracks; 1. of pottery, referring to a 'crazy paving' glaze effect caused by differences in rates of expansion/contraction between body and glaze; 2. of paintings, the mesh of cracks in paint or varnish similarly caused by differing shrinkage rates.

**cryselephantine** – name given to decorative sculptures executed in a combination of materials, such as bronze and ivory.

**delftware** – tin-glazed earthenwares (both *blue-and-white* and polychrome) made in the Low Countries or in England: the name honours the city of Delft as a major producer and influence on surrounding countries.

**dovetail** – V-shaped carpenter's joint used singly or in series, seen especially on Georgian furniture.

**dust wrapper** – also 'dust-cover' or 'dust-jacket', the protective jacket, usually of paper, printed with the book's title, author and an image, a 20th-century innovation.

**enamel** – coloured (translucent or opaque) glass: in metalwork fused within a prepared network of applied wires or within a carved/excavated field (= respectively cloisonné and champlevé techniques); in ceramics, pigments of coloured glass painted and fired on to a glazed or biscuit surface (see also *famille rose* and *famille verte*).

**faience** – *tin-glazed* earthenware from France or the Germanic countries.

**fake** – an object which has been modified (by addition or subtraction) in order to pass it off as something it isn't; term used more widely to include *forgery* (qv).

**famille rose** – literally 'pink family' – an enamel colour-scheme used on Chinese porcelain from *circa* 1720 comprising a distinctive pink (imported from Europe) while other colours are opacified by the addition of white: replacing the more translucent enamels of the '*famille verte*' colour scheme.

**famille verte** – literally 'green family' – a colour-scheme of translucent enamels used on Chinese porcelains essentially from the 15th century through to 1720 and revived in the 19th century.

**finial** – button, knop or knob applied as small handle or simple decoration to the top of an object (eg of a column, a piece of furniture or a teapot lid).

**forgery** – an object or piece of work that from the moment of manufacture was made to deceive, usually with a view to financial gain (see also *fake*).

**French polish** – hard, shiny, shellac lacquer applied to furniture from the late 18th century onwards, often obscuring colour and other natural properties of wood.

**fretted** – patterned with a geometric design of intersecting lines resembling a fence, trellis or lattice: open fretwork is cut right through, blind fretwork is left as an unpierced pattern in relief.

**gesso** – type of plaster containing chalk, suitable for complex carving and integration within ornamental wood frames intended for final gilding.

**glaze** – 1. In ceramics the glassy skin fired on to an earthenware, stoneware or porcelain body. A ceramic glaze may be transparent or stained (see also *tin-glaze*); 2. A varnish applied to an oil or watercolour painting.

**guilloche** – a platted motif usually in borders; term also describing a repeated motif engraved into silver or gold and flooded with enamel.

**hallmark** – a mark punched into silver indicating origin incorporating one or all (depending on country and era) of the following: date, maker, quality of metal and place (hall) of endorsement.

**hard-paste porcelain** – any porcelain whose recipe is based largely on two ingredients, china stone and china clay (petuntse and kaolin) – the formula developed in the Tang dynasty by the Chinese – and whose 'hardness' differs from the softer look of many European porcelains which may comprise altogether different ingredients. Most early English porcelains are *soft-paste*. Learning to distinguish hard from soft pastes is an important step to determining originals from copies.

**Humpen** – large cylindrical German drinking vessel, usually made of glass or silver.

**Imari** – Japanese port on the island of Kyushu through which most export porcelains from Arita were shipped: hence name given to Japanese porcelain decorated in distinctive *underglaze* blue, iron red and gold; and by onward association the name given to this palette wherever used (eg Royal Crown Derby).

**Kakiemon** – family name of Japanese potters associated with porcelain enamelled in a distinctive colour scheme usually including turquoise blue, a darker lapis blue, yellow, iron red and black enamels. But in fact produced from the mid-17th century onwards by several centres. Highly regarded by European collectors then and today: by extension this colour palette when used by any factory.

**knop** – the ornamental button or *finial* surmounting any vessel.

**kraak** – Dutch name for Portuguese *carrack* the vessels in which Chinese ceramics were traded from China in the 16th and 17th centuries: by extension, the name given to Chinese *blue-and-white* porcelain of that period and to the style (of repeated panels about a central scene) as copied by Japanese and European earthenware potters through the 17th century.

**lead crystal** – any glass whose formula includes lead oxide rendering it softer to cut and engrave and giving it a distinctive 'black' tinge when held up to the light.

**lion passant** – heraldic term for lion walking with right fore-paw raised.

**lion sejant** – heraldic term for seated lion.

**lustre-ware** – ceramic term for any metallic on-glaze effect seen variously from 9th century Near Eastern pottery to Hispano-Moresque (Spain), 16th-century Italian maiolica, 19th-century Staffordshire silver lustre, William de Morgan and modern studio potters.

**maiolica** – *tin-glazed* earthenwares from Italy and Spain, reaching an artistic peak in the 16th century: name derived from island of Majorca via which early wares (and the technology) were shipped to Italy: highly prized by 18th- and 19th-century collectors, and copied in 19th and 20th centuries. Not to be confused with *majolica*.

**majolica** – the brightly coloured, deeply moulded earthenwares made in Staffordshire from the 1840s and subsequently in the USA and France: name reflects the influence of similarly moulded and coloured *maiolica* wares of Italian Renaissance such as the della Robbia family.

**marquetry** – decoration in variously coloured wood veneers, (sometimes with ivory and metalwork elements) forming a picture or composition (eg depicting fruit, flowers or landscapes) usually inlaid into furniture or wood artefacts (see also *parquetry*).

**Meissen** – town in Saxony (Germany) first and subsequently foremost European porcelain manufacturer, the first to discover the Chinese secret formula for *hard-paste porcelain* (c.1710). In older English-language textbooks Meissen porcelain is referred to as 'Dresden', the Saxon capital through which much Meissen was marketed. Amongst the most copied of all porcelain wares as is its distinctive mark, a pair of crossed swords.

**metal** – of glass: term used to describe the fused ingredients or make-up of the glass material (a reference to its actual metal content).

**metaphysical artists** – name given to an Italian branch of the Surrealist movement, a group of artists including Giorgio de Chirico who, during and after World War I, depicted dream, subconscious and anxiety states.

**mould-blown** – any glass object whose form is achieved by its being blown (rather than pressed) into a mould.

**Neo-Classical** – revival of a Classical (antique Greek or Roman) style or Order: there have been many revivals of the shapes and forms of antiquity. In 18th century England Neo-Classicism, replacing the Rococo style around 1760, is associated with straight lines, symmetry and bands of repeated *ad infinitem* ornament such as *guilloche*, palmette and key-fret borders, as epitomized in the decorative schemes of the Adam family and their followers; the 18th-century Adam style was revived at the end of the Victorian era.

**netsuke** – a class of Japanese button from which a pouch or small box may be suspended: at first made of a natural root fragment netsuke were soon carved from any available material (most commonly wood and ivory) eventually becoming a miniature art-form: today highly prized, expensive and much faked.

**ormolu** – literally 'wrought gold': name given to high-quality Mercury gilt brasswork cast, tooled and chased into scrolls and *cartouches*, either as free-standing works (such as firedogs) or as mounts for expensive furniture and porcelain in the *Baroque, Rococo* and *Neo-Classical* styles of the 18th century. In the 19th century imitation mass-market 'ormolu' fittings became popular, executed in baser metals to a much lower quality.

**overglaze** – painted decoration applied to a ceramic glazed surface.

**pad feet** – pad-shaped foot (often at the base of a *cabriole* leg).

**parquetry** – similar to marquetry, though design purely geometrical.

**paste** – 1. name given to glass imitating gems; 2. raw porcelain clay body prior to being fired (see *hard-paste* and *soft-paste*).

**patina** – a colour and/or texture which develops naturally on any surface over time (owing to chemical reaction as well as wear) or which is artificially induced, whether or not to simulate age. Most bronzes are given a patina at the time of casting.

**Pinchbeck** – alloy of copper and zinc, resembling gold; named after inventor.

**platinotype** – a photographic process using platinum oxide giving an image closely resembling graphite pencil.

**porcelain** – European name given to ceramic body first developed in China in the Tang dynasty (618–906 AD) and imitated throughout the world in the centuries thereafter: its main qualities are whiteness and translucency: also referred to as 'china' though this term (as 'pottery') is also used generically to denote all ceramics.

**pre-Raphaelites** – name adopted by a group of mid-19th century English artists espousing a return to Italian painting styles and symbolism prior to the mannerism of Raphael.

**resin** – natural substance from trees or similar looking synthetic material lending itself to carving or casting.

**ring-turning** – rings (single or in clusters) turned on a lathe; usually on furniture or frameworks.

**Rococo** – an 18th-century style emerging from the more serious and symmetrical 17th-century Baroque style, its light-hearted asymmetric curves and scrolls imitating swirls, shells, leaves and the random play of water and rocaille (gnarled rock formations); gradually replaced by the Neo-Classical in the 1760s but revived in the 1830s.

**scroll** – a foliated flourish of serpentine or C-shaped outline.

**Sèvres** – the foremost French porcelain manufacturer based at town of same name; at first known as Vincennes (from ?1738) but changed to 'Sèvres' in 1753 on the official entry of Mme de Pompadour into the ownership of the factory: as with Meissen (which it also emulated) the Sèvres style is highly copied along with its mark of interlaced 'L's', and with several pieces sold *in the white* during and after the French Revolution, fakes abound.

**slipware** – pottery covered or decorated (or both) in slip, a coloured liquid clay.

**soda glass** – glass using sodium carbonate rather than potash as a flux (melting agent): a glass made of soda is not so resonant as one of *lead crystal*. Resonance is therefore a useful test in determining origin.

**soft-paste porcelain** – any porcelain (usually European) whose recipe differs from the Chinese so as to render the body more porous, the glaze less flinty. Many early European porcelains are 'soft' as factories experimented with various substances including flint, bone, feldspar, soap and soapstone.

**stoneware** – one of the three fundamental ceramic clay types the others being earthenware and porcelain. Fired to temperatures usually over 1,200°C, stoneware is hard, vitrified and impervious to water.

**strapwork** – ornamental design of strap-like bands running in and out, over and under, often in a more wanton way than *guilloche*.

**stretcher** – 1. a piece of wood acting as a strut or reinforcement between two other pieces (eg between the legs of a chair or table); 2. the frame upon which a painter's canvas is pinned.

**tenon joint** – 'a wood joint allowing two pieces to meet at an angle, one carved with a socket (= mortise) the other with a correspondingly shaped (usually rectangular) protuberance slotting into the mortise'.

**tin-glaze** – of pottery: a lead-based glaze rendered white with added ashes of tin, making an otherwise transparent glaze opaque and suitable for painting in one or several various metallic oxides: in current English textbooks tin-glazed earthenwares from Italy and Spain are usually called *maiolica*, from France and Germany *faience* or fayence and from the Low Countries and the British Isles, *delftware*.

**underglaze** – decoration painted, carved or applied direct on to a ceramic surface and subsequently glazed: one of the commonest forms of porcelain decoration being underglaze cobalt blue, known as *blue and white*.

**varnish** – oil or spirit-based liquid giving hard, clear finish to furniture.

**vellum** – kid or lamb skin used for pages and binding of early books.

**veneer** – thin sheet of wood used to cover a furniture carcass or for inlay effects (see *marquetry* and *parquetry*).

**watermark** – mark impregnated into paper as it is manufactured, often giving an exact date and therefore a useful age guide to the text or image.

**white, in the** – piece of uncoloured but glazed (ie not *biscuit*) porcelain.

**wove paper** – paper manufactured by a technique invented c.1755, being deposited on to a woven gauze rather than (as until then) being laid onto a mesh of thick and thinner wires (these being revealed as marks when held up to light).

# CONTRIBUTERS' BIOGRAPHIES

JON BADDELEY Six years after joining Sotheby's as a porter in 1971, Jon was running the Collectors' Department, following which he enjoyed a brief sojourn with a Covent Garden gallery specializing in English Fine and Decorative Arts. He rejoined Sotheby's in 1981 and is now Head of the Collectors' Division responsible for sales as diverse as classic cars, coins, stamps and musical instruments. He is a Director of the company and a regular auctioneer. His wide-ranging expertise includes scientific and medical instruments, automobilia, marine works of art, cameras and sporting memorabilia. He is the author of the reference work *Nautical Antiques and Collectables* and is a regular contributor to several specialist publications.

KEITH BAKER is an independent valuer and dealer, concentrating on all aspects of late 19th- and 20th-century Decorative Arts, having been the Head of the Art Nouveau & Decorative Arts Department at Phillips Auctioneers, London, for 23 years. Working initially as a photographer then in computers, he joined Sotheby's European & Oriental Ceramics Departments before moving to Phillips in 1976. He regularly lectures in the UK and internationally, having a particular interest in silver, jewellery and accessories from 1860 to the present day.

DAVID BATTIE is a specialist in Ceramics and Oriental Works of Art and lectures widely to groups and societies throughout the land. He trained as a graphic designer and worked for three years at Reader's Digest before joining Sotheby's in 1967 as a book porter. He became a director in 1976 and married the company's glass expert, Sarah Francis. He has written and edited numerous books – including several price guides to 19th century pottery and porcelain – and has been on *The Antiques Roadshow* from the very first series in 1979. On retiring from Sotheby's he became editor of the Arts Magazine *Masterpiece.*

JOHN BENJAMIN served his apprenticeship at Cameo Corner, the Bloomsbury antique jewellers. In 1976, he joined Phillips Fine Art Auctioneers as a junior cataloguer, ultimately becoming responsible for the auctions taking place in London, Geneva and New York. John is now an independent jewellery advisor and lecturer specializing in the Renaissance, 18th- and 19th-century periods. He is a fellow of the Gemmological Association and consultant to the National Association of Goldsmiths Registered Valuers Scheme.

SOPHIE DUPRÉ started her career in publishing. After being asked to organize the sale of a large collection of 19th-century literary letters, she emerged into the world of antiques with autographs, letters, manuscripts and literary property as a strong interest. She joined the autograph department of Francis Edwards Ltd in London. In 1983 she left to settle in Wiltshire where she brings up her young family while continuing to run a successful business selling autograph letters and manuscripts to institutions and private collectors. She is one of the world's leading experts in royal manuscripts.

CLIVE FARAHAR is a specialist in fine and rare books. He served his apprenticeship at one of London's old established antiquarian booksellers, Francis Edwards Ltd, becoming a partner in 1979. Now in private practice, he lectures at London University on the Post Graduate course in Antiquarian Bookselling and he also writes articles on the subject.

IAN HARRIS For many years Ian Harris has run the family silver and jewellery business, N. Bloom & Son, in London. In his youth he received a thorough grounding in English antique silver, old Sheffield and Victorian plate, carriage clocks and bronzes. In the 1960s, the firm diversified into old jewellery, now its major interest. Ian has written two books on silver and is a Freeman of the Worshipful Company of Goldsmiths and of the City of London. He has been on the *Antiques Roadshow* team from the beginning and before that appeared on *Going for a Song* with Arthur Negus. He has taught himself heraldry in order to look up armorials on antique silver and jewellery, and he is a keen collector of both paintings and decorative objects related to the octopus.

HILARY KAY started her career in antiques with Spink & Son, fine art dealers of St James's, and left to join Sotheby's in 1977. Soon after, she became Head of the Collectors' Department and one of the first women auctioneers. She specialized in scientific instruments, toys, automata, dolls, mechanical musical instruments and rock and roll memorabilia. She was appointed Senior Director of Sotheby's in 1990 and became responsible for seven departments ranging from motor cars and fine wines to postage stamps and scientific instruments. Hilary regularly broadcasts, lectures and writes on the subjects of antiques and collectables. She has also edited a general guidebook to British antiques and is the author of *Rock and Roll Collectables* – an illustrated history of rock memorabilia.

RUPERT MAAS is a fine art dealer working from his gallery in the West End of London. The gallery specializes in Pre-Raphaelite and English Romantic pictures and was started by his father, Jeremy Maas, in the 1960s. Rupert has organized a number of important exhibitions at the gallery (John Ruskin and his circle; Pre-Raphaelites and Romantics; Victorian Paintings; British Illustrators; Burne-Jones; Victorian fairy paintings). He studied art history at Essex University and is a past Chairman of the Young National Art-Collections Fund. He is responsible for co-organizing an annual trade fair in London called the Watercolours and Drawings Fair and he is also a member of the Executive Committee of the society of London Art Dealers.

LARS THARP is a regular member of the BBC *Antiques Roadshow* team, specializing in Ceramics and Oriental Works of Art. As expert/presenter he appears on many TV antiques and Arts programmes as well as being chairman-quizmaster of BBC Radio Four's *Hidden Treasures*. He has written, edited and contributed to several books including *Treasures in Your Home* (with David Battie), *The Little Brown Encyclopedia of Antiques* (with Paul Atterbury) and *Hogarth's China*, a tribute to William Hogarth. Born in Copenhagen, Lars was educated in England, reading Archaeology at Cambridge whereafter becoming an auctioneer and Director at Sotheby's. He divides his time between lecturing, broadcasting and running his own Ceramics and Fine Art Consultancy.

PETER WALDRON is a Senior Director of Sotheby's and is responsible for silver, *objets de vertu* and portrait miniatures in the UK and Europe. He joined the firm in 1966 as a Junior Administrator, transferring two years later to the Silver Department as cataloguer. He is author of *The Price Guide to Antique Silver* and contributes articles to specialist magazines. He is also an enthusiast in British heraldic researches and identifications. He is a Liveryman of the Worshipful Company of Goldsmiths, a member of the Antique Plate Committee of Goldsmiths Hall, Freeman of the City of London and a member of the Silver Society since 1978.

TIM WONNACOTT is a third generation auctioneer. He joined Sotheby's in 1978 and has recently been appointed Chairman of Sotheby's South, based at Billingshurst in Sussex. His specialist subjects include furniture, clocks and works of art and he is a Fellow of the Royal Institute of Chartered Surveyors and an Associate of the Society of Valuers and Auctioneers. He regularly contributes to a wide range of antiques publications and is a familiar face on many antiques programmes, including BBC2's *The Antiques Show* and *The Antiques Inspectors*.

The authorship of individual articles can be found on page 192.

# BIBLIOGRAPHY

Anderson, Basil *Gem Testing*.

Becker, Vivienne *Antique and 20th Century Jewellery*.

Bennett, David & Daniella Mascetti *Understanding Jewellery*.

Bernard, Philippa, Leo Bernard and Angus O'Neill *Antiquarian Books – A Companion for Booksellers, Librarians and Collectors*, 1994.

Bruton, Eric *Diamonds*.

Carter, J. *ABC for Book Collectors*, 1952 and revised editions.

Carter, J. and others *Printing and the Mind of Man. A Descriptive Catalogue Illustrating the Impact of Print on the Evolution of Western Civilization during Five Centuries*, 1967.

Carter, J. & G. Pollard *An Enquiry into the Nature of Certain Nineteenth Century Pamphlets*, 1934.

Darlow, T. H. & H.F. Moule *Historical Catalogue of the Printed Editions of Holy Scripture in the Library of the British and Foreign Bible Society*, 4 vols, 1904. Vol. 1 *English Bibles* revised and expanded by A. S. Herbert, 1968.

Freeston, Ewart *Prisoner of War Ship Models* (London), 1973.

Hamilton, *Charles Great Forgers and Famous Fakes*.

Hamilton, Charles *Collecting Autographs and Manuscripts*. Harvey, Brian W. *Violin Fraud* (Clarendon Press, Oxford) 1992.

Henderson, Ian T. & David Stirk *Golf in the Making* (London), 1979.

Jones, Mark (ed.) *Fake? The Art of Deception* (British Museum Exhibition Catalogue, London) 1990.

Kurz, Otto *Fakes – A Handbook for Collectors and Students* (Faber & Faber, London) 1948.

Le Grand, Michel *Mascottes Automobiles*.

Munn, Geoffrey *Jewellery Pre-Raphaelite to Arts and Crafts*.

Olman, John & Morton *Encyclopaedia of Golf Collectibles* (Alabama), 1985.

Rendell, Kenneth *Forging History*.

Rendell, Kenneth *History Comes to Life*.

Rudoe, Judy *Cartier 1900–1939*.

Schüller, Sepp *Forgers, Dealers, Experts* (English translation, Arthur Barker, London) 1960.

Stuart, Frank *Dictionary of Scrimshaw Artists* (Mystic Sea Port), 1991.

Thomas, Alan *Great Books and Book Collectors*, 1975.

Turner, Gerard L. *Nineteenth Century Scientific Instruments* (London), 1983.

William, C. William *Motoring Mascots of the World*.

# INDEX

# ACKNOWLEGDEMENTS

## Photographic credits

t = top, c = centre, b = bottom, l = left, r = right

6t, 7b, 16–17, 19tl, 22l, 22r, 23l, 23r, 24l, 24r, 25l, 25r, 26l, 27tl, 27tr, 27b, 29t, 29b, 31t, 31b, 33, 35t, 35b, 36, 37t, 37b, 38, 39t, 39b, 41l, 41r, 47, 53l, 53r, 54l, 54r, 55l, 55r, 161, 162, 163l, 163r, 166 David Battie; 6ct, 64l, 65r, 66l, 66r, 67l, 67r The Board of Trustees of the National Museums & Galleries on Merseyside (Lady Lever Art Gallery); 6cb, 72–3, 75l, 75r, 79, 82t, 82b, 83 The Maas Gallery Ltd; 6b, 12t, 94, 95, 96, 97, 98, 99 Leapfrog Press Ltd; 7t, 7cb, 13t, 14b, 15b, 18, 19bl, 19r, 20, 21t, 21c, 21b, 34l, 34r, 40, 45b, 70, 102, 104–5, 106, 107, 108l, 108r, 109l, 109r, 110, 111t, 111c, 111b, 112, 113t, 113b, 114l, 114r, 115, 116, 117, 118, 119, 120t, 120ct, 120cb, 120b, 121t, 121b, 122, 123l, 123r, 124, 125tl, 125tr, 125b, 136–7, 138t, 138b, 146t, 146c, 146b, 147, 148t, 148cl, 148cr, 148b, 149t, 149b, 150t, 150b, 151, 152, 153, 154t, 154b, 155t, 155b, 156, 157t, 157b Sotheby's, London; 7ct, 10, 14t, 28, 48, 52, 80, 88, 89, 90–91, 93, 134t, 134b, 160 Bridgeman Art Library; 11t, 58, 59t, 59b, 60t, 60b, 61t, 61b, 62t, 62b, 63l, 63tr, 63br, 64r, 65l, 68l, 68r, 69l, 69r, 71t, 71b Tim Wonnacott; 11b, 86, 87 Popperfoto; 12b, 164, 165l, 165r Robert Kleiner & Co. Ltd; 13t Anne Stabler Associates; 15t, 100 Scala; 32 British Museum; 42 The Potteries Museum, Stoke-on-Trent; 43t, 43b, 44, 45t, 49 Lars Tharp; 50t, 50b, 51t Staffordshire County Council; 51b, 56–7 © Christie's Images; 74 Musée de l'impression sur étoffes, Mulhouse; 76 ET Archive; 77 AKG Photo © Christie's/AKG; 78 City of Plymouth Museums & Art Gallery; 84 Popperfoto/Reuter; 85, 126–7 © AKG London; 128 The Trustees of the Victoria & Albert Museum, London; 129l, 158–9, 168 Phillips, London; 129r, 133, 135 John Benjamin; 130 tl, 130cl, 130bl, 130r, 131 N. Bloom & Son; 132 Tessiers; 139l, 139r, 143 © Clive Corless; 140, 141, 142t, 142b, 144 © AALCS; 169, 170, 171, 173t, 173b Keith Baker; 172 Alastair Carew-Cox.

## Text credits

9 Foreword © Hugh Scully; 10–15 Introduction, 16–17 Pottery, Porcelain and Glass, 20–21 Chenghua Period Chicken Cup, 32–3 A Maiolica Plate, 40–41 Vienna Porcelain, 42–3 Toft Slipware Dish, 44–5 Chelsea Rabbit Tureen, 48–9 Bernard Leach Pottery, 50–51 Carlton Ware, 156–7 Stradivarius Violins, 158–9 Other Works of Art, 160–61 Far Eastern Bronzes, 162–3 Masatsugu Netsuke and Okimono, 164–5 Snuff Bottles, 166–7 Billies and Charlies © Lars Tharp; 18–19 Ming Vase, 22–5 Kraak, 26–7 Imari Vases, 28–9 *Famile Rose* Tobacco-leaf Bowl, 30–31 A Chinese Export 'Scotsman' Plate, 34–5 Meissen Figure of Avvocato, 36–7 Herold-Decorated Porcelain, 38–9 Sèvres Jewelled Cup and Saucer, 46–7 A Bow Quail Pattern Dish, 52–3 Early Lead Glass, 54–5 Humpen © David Battie; 56–7 Furniture, 58–9 Georgian Stool, 60–61 Gainsborough Armchair, 62–3 Carved Giltwood Mirrors, 64–5 Chinese Chippendale Armchair, 66–7 Classical Commode, 68–9 *Bonheur du Jour*, 70–71, A Georgian Quartetto of Tables © Tim Wonnacott; 72–3 Paintings, Drawings and Sculpture, 74–5 Benner Still-life, 76–7 Van Gogh's *Sunflowers*, 78–9 *Study for the Masque of Cupid*, 80–81 Frith's *The Railway Station*, 82–3 Marble Relief of Nelson, 84–7 Han van Meegeren, 88–9 Tom Keating © Rupert Maas; 90–91 Books and Manuscripts, 92–3 Famous Manuscript Forgeries, 94–5 Facsimile Letters, 96–7 The Autopen, 99–9 The Book Forgeries of Thomas J. Wise, 100–101 Early Bookbindings, 102–3 Dustwrappers © Sophie Dupré and Clive Farahar; 104–5 Silver, 106–11 Metamorphoses, 112–13 Coffee Pots, 114–15 Tankards and Mugs, 116–19 Early Spoons, 120–21 Silver Bowls, 122–3 Rococo Soup Tureen, 124–5 Nuremberg Beakers © Peter Waldron; 126–7 Precious Objects, 128–9 Renaissance Pendant, 132–3 Fabergé Objet d'Art, 134–5 Paste © John Benjamin; 130–31 Diamond Jewellery © Ian Harris; 136–7 Collectables, 138–9 Automata, 140–41 Bisque-headed Doll, 142–3 Steiff Teddy Bear, 144–5 Cast-iron Money Banks © Hilary Kay; 146–7 Feathery Golf Balls, 148–9 Scrimshaw, 150–51 Prisoner-of-War Ship Models, 152–3 Motoring Mascots, 154–5 Box Sextants © Jon Baddeley; 168–9 Gallé Cameo Glass Vase, 170–71 Bronze and Ivory Figure, 172–3 Christopher Dresser Vase © Keith Baker.